SHINGLE STYLE

155 Home Plans from Classic Colonials to Breezy Bungalows

HOME PLANNERS, LLC
Wholly owned by Hanley-Wood, LLC
TUCSON ARIZONA

SHINGLE STYLE

Published by Home Planners, LLC
Wholly owned by Hanley-Wood, LLC
3275 W. Ina Road, Suite 110
Tucson, Arizona 85741

Distribution Center:
29333 Lorie Lane
Wixom, Michigan 48393

Patricia Joseph, President
Jan Prideaux, Editor In Chief
Kristin Schneidler, Editor
Prairie Markussen, Plans Editor
Paul Fitzgerald, Senior Graphic Designer
Teralyn Morriss, Graphic Production Artist

Photo Credits
Front Cover: Design HPT150004, see page 23. Photo provided by Stephen Fuller, Inc.
Back Cover: Design HPT150002, see page 13. Photo by Russell Kingman, Home Design Services

10 9 8 7 6 5 4 3 2 1

Printed in the United States of America

Library of Congress Catalog Card Number: 00-111870
ISBN softcover: 1-881955-85-0

CONTENTS

Design HPT150001, see page 17.

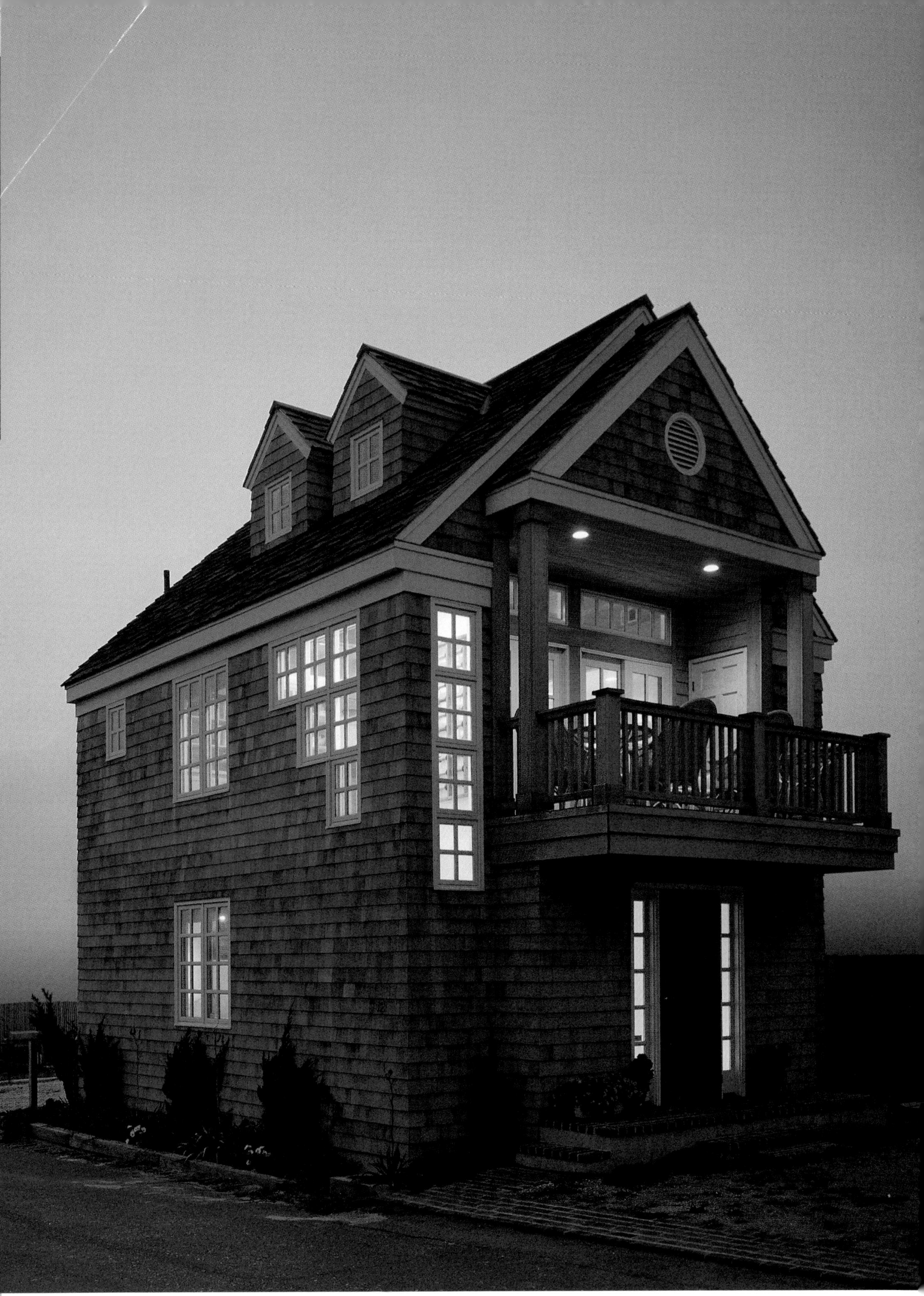

EDITOR'S NOTE

The current interest in traditional neighborhood design—a new sort of urban planning based on older towns, with a mix of many architectural styles—has also sparked a general curiosity about traditional building materials. Shingles, which have long been a part of American architectural tradition, have experienced several surges in popularity, from early Colonial days to the 1920s and 1930s. Today, the warmth, character and sense of easy living that shingles add to a home has caused them to once again become a sought-after building material. No doubt their versatility—shingles complement a wide variety of architectural styles—is a factor in their increasing popularity.

The following collection of plans includes more than 150 designs featuring shingle cladding and accents. Following a full-color showcase of some of today's best-selling plans, the sections are conveniently arranged by style. Beginning with Cape Cod and Early Colonial designs, moving through country and European-style cottages, Craftsman homes, Victorian and farmhouse designs, and ending with breezy coastal homes and vacation cottages, this book offers a look at the history of shingle design in America. Take a moment to browse through this comprehensive collection; you'll find home plans that combine the traditions of the past with the carefully planned, amenity-filled interiors of the new century.

*Design HPT150017;
see page 37.*

HISTORY

Shingles were commonly used as an exterior cladding material in Colonial America; according to some authorities, the use of shingles originated with the Dutch on Long Island. If this is so, the idea must have caught on rapidly, for many houses on Nantucket adopted it before 1700. The 17th-Century Jethro Coffin House on the island is a notable example. Shingles were also made in Connecticut in 1639.

Shingles afforded the early Dutch, Swedish and English settlers an easier means to sheath a house than did clapboard siding, which required much effort to saw. In the late 1700s, it became common practice for people to clapboard the front of their house, but shingle the ends and back (see illustration).

Most of these early shingles were made from white pine, up to three feet long and ten inches wide. They were split rough, then finished slightly with a drawknife. Having the natural grooves on the surfaces, they shed water better than the smooth-sawn ones—a fact that undoubtedly accounts for their long life. Some shingles were given an occasional coat of whitewash in their earlier years.

Later, shingles were typically split from logs of cedar or cypress. The bandsaw, perfected after the Civil War, made it easy to turn out shingles of any desired shape. Carpenters used this resource to invent a fertile repertory of shingle shapes inspired by many sources—for example, the round shingle appearance derives from fish scales. With the new shingle types available, shingles were used on more houses in a wider range of styles.

The years immediately following the Civil War brought a new prosperity to many American families. Prior to the war, the economy had revolved around agriculture; most people worked long hours and had little leisure time. The growth of heavy industry and manufacturing changed this, allowing some people to devote time to leisurely pursuits. Weekends and summers became times for wealthy, and even simply prosperous, families to take vacations to the forests, mountains and seashores. These groups of people began to wish for a new sort of architecture: an architecture that created carefree, easy feelings, that reflected the past but looked to the future as well.

SHINGLE STYLE

In 1874, the inaugural issue of **The New York Sketchbook of Architecture** contained a photograph of Whitehall, the Bishop George Berkeley House in Middletown, Rhode Island, which had been built in 1728-29. The photo, a rear view, showed a house that appeared to be entirely clad in wooden shingles. Editors included it in hopes of promoting a new, uniquely American approach to design, one that took advantage of the flexibility and lightness of wood.

This photograph admirably served its purpose. In the four years following its appearance, designers did indeed take a fresh look at American architecture and traditions. A new style, one that borrowed from several others, arose—the Shingle style.

The Shingle style flourished in oceanfront resorts of the northeastern states between 1880 and 1900, with a few examples of the late 1870s and early 1900s. Popular vacation destinations such as Newport, Cape Cod, eastern Long Island and Coastal Maine offered many representations of the style, some of which still stand today. The Newport Casino serves as one example; the Kingscote Dining Room, also in Newport, is another. Though these buildings were actually social centers, most examples of the Shingle style were architect-designed cottages and homes made for those wealthy Americans who had desired an easy, carefree architecture. In this style's heyday, they were popular as the comfortable, fashionable dwelling places of the **nouveau riche**.

Since the Shingle style is an adaptation of several other architectural traditions, it can be a hard style to pin down. It borrowed primarily from three other design styles: Queen Anne, Colonial Revival and Richardson Romanesque. The combination of the wide porches and asymmetrical facades of the Queen Anne style, the gambrel roofs, lean-to additions and classical columns of Colonial Revival homes and the arches, stone lower stories and irregular, sculpted shapes of the Richardson Romanesque style made Shingle-style homes an unusually free-form and variable architecture. Shingle-style homes were also influenced by Japanese and Medieval English architecture, and many of the

Design HPT150145, a modern-day Shingle-style home; see page 169.

Design HPT150016, a time-honored Cape Cod home; see page 36.

interiors featured Japanese decorative motifs. The Shingle style remained a high-fashion architect's style, thereby allowing for its great range of variation; it was never adapted to mass vernacular housing as another style, the Queen Anne Victorian, was.

The influence of the Shingle style is apparent, though—builders, inspired by the well-publicized originals, put up their own more modest versions in many late 19th-Century suburbs. Adaptations also arose in the Pacific Northwest, perhaps because of convenient access to raw materials. With natural colors predominating, the Shingle style was likewise promoted by the Arts and Crafts movement as a "back to nature" building idiom. From this base, well publicized in contemporary architectural magazines, the style spread throughout the country, and scattered examples can be found today in all regions.

The recent trend towards traditionally styled homes has generated a resurgence of interest in the Shingle style, especially in the regions where it was once so popular. For many people, it will always be, as Vincent Scully describes it, "the architecture of the American summer." Shingles themselves, last popular as an exterior cladding material in the 1920s and 1930s, are now making a comeback as well.

STYLE COUNSEL

The style of a house is an important determinant of the exterior material used on the home. A Cape Cod home would not be fully authentic if it was built with stucco walls, for example, and a Spanish-style home would not look as genuine if it were clad in shingles. The following guide defines several popular architectural styles that typically are clad in, or accented by, shingles. These styles include Cape Cod, Early Colonial, Craftsman/Bungalow, and Victorian.

Cape Cod Style

The delightful Cape Cod cottage, cute and quaint, started life as a down-to-earth shelter for early Colonists and over the years became an American synonym for comfort. Easy to build and maintain, generally inexpensive to heat and just right for remodeling, the Cape Cod has long been a popular American housing style.

Style Points

The Cape Cod design that Americans have grown to know and love has several distinctive characteristics.

■ **Basic Box** Like other housing styles that date to the Colonial era, Cape Cods are very straightforward. Their simplicity makes them splendid candidates for additions and full-scale remodeling projects.

■ **1½ stories** The earliest Capes were one-story houses, but quickly developed into the definitive 1½-story type. Traditionally, bedrooms were on the first floor, with the half-story representing space for growing families in need of an extra bedroom. Modern Capes generally have at least one bed and bath upstairs.

■ **Steeply Pitched, Side-Gabled Roof** Gables are triangular parts of a wall formed by the intersection of two pitched roof plans. Most Cape Cods have gables facing the side, fairly steep roofs and undecorated eaves that link

them to their Colonial relatives. However, many Capes also display two or more front-facing dormers set into the roof.

■ **Shutters** Exterior shutters were not part of the 17th-Century Capes, but by the end of the 18th Century they had become regular additions and have remained so to this day. Cape Cod shutters always match the length of a window, which is typically a double-hung style.

■ **Central Entry** Plenty of Capes do not have central entries, but most of the modestly sized examples do. Contemporary Cape Cods often borrow details such as sidelights, transoms, crowns and pilasters from Georgian-style doors.

Early Colonial Style

When the Colonists arrived in America, they relied on familiar building techniques carried over from England, modified to meet the demands of the New World. Supported by post-and-beam construction, houses were small boxes, either one or two stories high and usually just a single room deep. They had steeply pitched gable or gambrel roofs covered by wood shingles, tiny windows with diamond-shaped panes, board-and-batten doors, and usu-

Design HPT150019, a refreshingly simple, symmetrical Colonial home; see page 39.

ally wood exterior walls, brick being a more expensive building material. Contemporary recreations of Early Colonial style are, of course, much larger than their predecessors, and most are supported by platform frames rather than posts and beams. However, carefully crafted renditions retain many of the exterior features.

Style Points
The best examples are attractively simple.

- **Basic Box** Floor plans echo 17th-Century design: simple rectangles, with the kitchen centered and to the rear.
- **Large Chimney with Decorative Top** To Colonists, immense fireplaces were the only way to keep warm and cook food. Though fireplaces are no longer a survival necessity, many early Colonial adaptations include fireplaces and employ one or more oversized chimneys. Colonial chimneys were often ornamented by intricate brickwork and decorative clay pots, made popular by the Tudor style in England.
- **Overhanging Upper Story** As with many other features, 17th-Century Colonists borrowed an overhang, or jetty, from Medieval English building traditions, which often called for an upper floor that projected over the street. The resulting style is often dubbed "garrison house,"

though any Colonist would have used the term more precisely to describe a true frontier outpost.

- **Board Door** Throughout most of the 17th Century, doors were rigidly utilitarian—heavy planks set vertically in a simple surround and joined by wood battens. These austere entries were replaced by the paneled doors of the Georgian style, which were often highlighted by pilasters and sidelights.

Craftsman and Bungalow Style
Craftsman style was dominant from around 1905 to the early 1920s; it was the main style for smaller houses built throughout the country. It originated in Southern California, and many examples of Craftsman architecture are still concentrated there. Inspired by the work of two brothers—Charles Sumner Greene and Henry Mather Greene—the style became popular through pattern books and magazines. Craftsman architecture was influenced by the Arts and Crafts movement and also by certain styles of Asian wooden architecture.

Style Points
Craftsman and bungalow-style homes are identified by a variety of prominent features.

The Craftsman style is easily recognizable. Design HPT150040, see page 61.

Fish-scale shingles lend charm to this Folk Victorian home. Design HPT150095; see page 118.

■ **One Story** Due to a flood of pattern books featuring one-story Craftsman and Bungalow designs, these houses quickly became the most fashionable small houses in the country in the early days of the style. Many of today's examples are two-story; however, they are still able to incorporate other identifying characteristics.

■ **Low-Pitched, Gabled Roof** A sharp contrast to the steeply pitched roofs of the Cape Cod and Early Colonial styles, Craftsman homes showcase low-pitched roofs, usually with a wide, unenclosed eave overhang and exposed rafter tails. Decorative beams and braces are often added under gables.

■ **Distinctive Porches** Porches can be either full- or partial-width, with the roof supported by tapered square columns and in some cases stone piers. Porch columns often extend to ground level, without a break in the porch floor.

■ **Mixed Exterior Materials** Wood clapboard and shingles are the two most common wall cladding for Craftsman homes; however, these materials are often mixed with stone, brick, concrete block or stucco to create eye-catching facades.

Victorian Style

Victorian architecture is actually an array of related styles, and is best characterized by asymmetrical shapes, multiple projections (overhangs, bay windows and wall insets), contrasting materials and exuberant details. "Less is more" was *not* the Victorian maxim. Contemporary adaptations often rely on a particular style that was immensely popular during the last two decades of the 19th Century. Called Queen Anne (after the early 18th-Century monarch), it actually had little to do with the formal, restrained architecture during her reign. Instead, Victorian Queen Anne houses were an appealing eclectic mix of architectural features and details. Transported by national magazines and transcontinental railroads, the style enchanted late 19th-Century homebuilders. Today's versions, among the hottest designs around, retain much of the attractively unique look of their historical predecessors.

Style Points

■ **Asymmetrical, Two-Story Facade** Classic Queen Annes were two-story houses that had marvelous, diversely detailed, unbalanced facades. Roof shapes varied considerably and usually featured multiple gables.

■ **Contrasting Wall Materials** Dramatic combinations of different materials and textures were signature traits of 19th-Century Queen Annes, and contemporary Victorians often echo the effect. Differing wall textures were commonly achieved with patterned wood shingles shaped into a variety of designs. A variety of materials was also used on the different stories of Queen Anne houses (shingle over clapboard or brick is most common).

■ **Color** The Victorians shunned white houses: they were too glowing and conspicuous. Traditionally, Victorian houses were painted subdued and natural colors, from soft pastels to olives, earthy browns, deep reds and dark greens. The brightly colored Victorians popular today were a 1960s adaptation originating in San Francisco.

■ **One-Story Porch** Spacious porches are a distinctive characteristic of Queen Anne style. The porch covered much or all of the front facade of the house, including the entrance. Porches have rebounded in popularity and are becoming an endearing feature of contemporary Victorian houses.

■ **Spindlework** More than half the original Queen Anne homes built in the United States displayed lacy, ornamental spindlework (turned wood elements). Also called "gingerbread," it typically appeared in porch balustrades and friezes, at gable ends and under bays.

Due to a revival in popularity, shingle cladding adds its warmth and charm to several of today's well-known home styles. Among them are the cozy cottages and comfortable farmhouses of the American country; these are joined by some larger European chateau-style and estate homes. Even some traditional homes display gables accented by shingles—and, of course, many of today's coastal and vacation homes showcase shingle cladding.

Shingles, particularly those made of cedar, are a sensible choice for an exterior cladding material. They require little maintenance, beyond staining at installation; they are also quite durable, often lasting over fifty years. However, they do take time to install correctly—if you choose the carefree, comfortable look of shingles for your home, select an experienced contractor who will install them properly.

Design HPT150041, a carefree coastal home; see page 165.

DESIGN HPT150002

Photos by Russell Kingman, Home Design Services

Design HPT150002 combines a charming shingle-and-siding exterior with a thoughtful floor plan that allows this home to live larger than its 1,997 square feet. Front-porch columns frame the elegantly decorated double doors of the entry, which open to the foyer. Inside, more columns define the dining room to the right of the foyer, while a powder room and coat closet offer convenience for visitors. Just beyond the powder room, double doors open to a den/study, where built-in bookshelves line one wall and a closet provides some extra storage space.

The plan's open layout allows easy movement between the fami-

Soaring ceilings and an open layout give this modestly sized cottage the appearance of a luxury home.

This home, as shown in the photographs, may differ from the actual blueprints.
For more detailed information, please check the floor plans carefully.

Above: A triple window brings natural light to the elegantly decorated breakfast room.

Left: Books, plants and unique accent pieces fill the built-in shelves in the study.

ly room, dining room and kitchen; each of these rooms provides special amenities. Three tall windows bring natural light into the dining room, while the kitchen features a central island, a pantry and a sensible entrance to the utility room. A snack bar, angled towards the family room, allows the cook to participate in family conversations. A vaulted ceiling, a fireplace and a built-in media center further enhance the family room. A covered patio, accessible from the family room and a snug eating nook, might serve as an outdoor dining area during balmy weather. The nook also opens to a greenhouse.

Another of this home's enjoyable features is the split-bedroom plan, which creates privacy for all family members. The master suite resides in the right wing, shielded from street noise by the two-car garage. A spacious walk-in closet and a full bath with a compartmented toilet make this a

Above: The thoughtfully arranged kitchen, highlighted by honey-toned cabinetry, includes a central work island.

Left: Natural light from the windows above the plant shelf further enhances the kitchen and family room.

truly luxurious retreat. A secondary bedroom sits to the left of the family room, with easy access to a hall bath. Additional space above the garage can be converted to a second family bedroom with a private bath.

Natural shades—beige, cream, pale yellow, white and cool green—blend with the honeyed tones of the wooden cabinetry and floors to create a muted, yet refreshing, color palette for this interior. These gentle hues meld with skillful interior lighting, making the rooms seem even larger. Simple earth-toned accent pieces set off carefully chosen furniture, while a wide variety of plants brings a hint of the outdoors into each room.

The opulent master bath showcases a generously sized shower and a step-up tub, which sits in an alcove overlooking the garden.

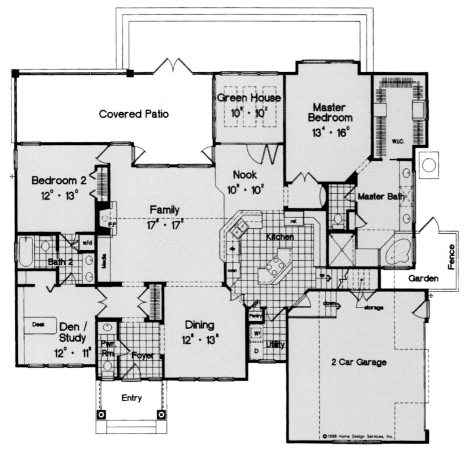

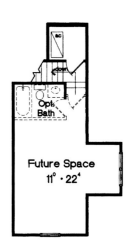

DESIGN HPT150002

Square Footage: 1,997
Bonus Space: 310 sq. ft.
Width: 64'-4"
Depth: 63'-0"

Design by
©Home Design
Services, Inc.

Interior Design: Garren, McCuan, Renner
Photography: Maguire Photographics

Tall windows, wicker furnishings and cool blue tones add to the country air of the great room.

This home, as shown in the photographs, may differ from the actual blueprints. For more detailed information, please check the floor plans carefully.

Design HPT150001 combines the best of European influences with rustic design, creating a truly unique and exciting plan. The exterior is comprised of cedar shake shingles, set off with delicate white trim and black shutters. Inviting flower boxes adorn several front-facing windows and serve to lend this home a cheery air. Black French-style shutters accent some of the white-trimmed muntin windows, while keystone lintel arches complement others. A white-painted wooden bench is positioned before the door, perfect for quiet repose before entering the house. The front door is black, framed in white decorative trim and topped with a beautiful sunburst window, allowing light to flow into the foyer.

Step into the foyer, flanked on the

DESIGN **HPT150001**

Wicker baskets, honey-toned wood and white-painted cabinets bring cheerful country style to the kitchen.

right side by a dining room which has convenient access to the kitchen. The curved, paneled ceiling of the foyer lends a port-town feel to this home right from the beginning. To the left of the foyer is a vaulted study, complete with a charming fireplace, creating an ideal place to enjoy a cozy read. Double doors to the study allow for privacy and quiet even when the rest of the house is full of noise. The vaulted great room is to the rear of the plan, past the stairs, and also boasts a fireplace. Cool tones and wood floors grace the great room, as does a room-size decorative rug, perfect for keeping warm during the winter months. A wall of windows and French doors allow an abundance of light to permeate, as well as providing easy access to the large rear deck. White wooden shutters attached to the French doors lend a sense of country to this room and also protect against too much light and heat. A palm tree and other plants add color to this seemingly cool-toned room and complement the blue and cream shades of the furniture and walls. Simple decorative touches seem to be the key to this room's success. An attractive mirror and decorative plates adorn one of the walls, while plain wood and wrought iron end tables accommodate visitors. A white wooden cabinet with gold knobs further accents the country influence in this home. An arched hallway—lined with pictures and a grandfather clock—leads elegantly from the great room into the

kitchen. Throughout the home, decorative cantilevers provide an antique feel to this otherwise modern home.

Wicker furniture, mixed with more refined styles, allows this home to be both comfortable and elegant. A repeating theme throughout the interior of this design is the mixture of white-painted wood furniture, offset by natural wood and accented by blues, blacks and greens present in the furniture and accessories. The kitchen is a cook's haven as it provides a tremendous amount of counter space, as well as a marble-topped food-preparation island. The cupboards are white, while counter tops and floor are natural wood. The paneled style of the cupboard doors matches the paneling of ceilings in other rooms, creating a sense of flow and continuity throughout the home. The sink and bar area overlooks the sunlit vaulted breakfast nook, complete with a simple country chandelier. The breakfast nook offers access to the deck and is a perfect spot for basking in the flood of light coming through the abundance of windows. A spacious laundry room is accessible from the kitchen and the two-car garage.

The first-floor master bedroom is set aside from the rest of the family bedrooms for maximum privacy and comfort. Well-lit and comfortably large, this bedroom also provides deck access. Elegantly adorned with a tray ceiling, this bedroom boasts a bay window sitting area, fit for a chaise lounge or small couch. The master bath boasts a garden

Above: An elegant armoire is the focal point of the master bedroom, which is further enhanced by a bay window and tray ceiling.

Left: Built-in bookshelves and a vaulted ceiling highlight the secluded study.

tub, separate shower, compartmented toilet, dual-vanities and access to His and Hers closets. An additional half-bath situated near the study completes the first floor.

Sprawling bedrooms and open spaces characterize the second floor. Bedroom 4 is enhanced with a walk-in closet, while Bedroom 3 is bathed in light with the abundance of windows available. Bedroom 2 boasts access to a flower box and ample closet space. A full hall bath, complete with double basins, is shared by the three family bedrooms. The second floor overlooks to the great room and foyer below, providing a sense of increased spaciousness to this lovely home.

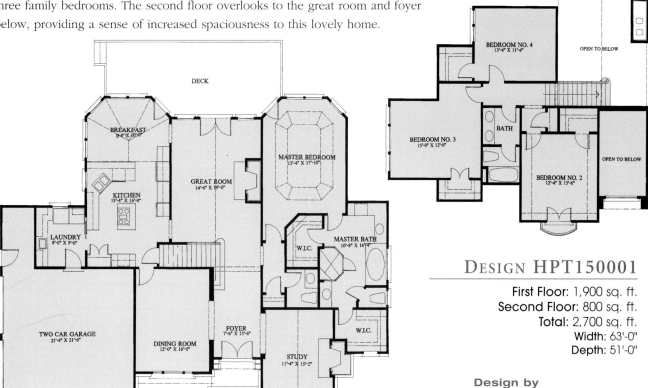

DESIGN HPT150001

First Floor: 1,900 sq. ft.
Second Floor: 800 sq. ft.
Total: 2,700 sq. ft.
Width: 63'-0"
Depth: 51'-0"

Design by
©Stephen Fuller, Inc.

DESIGN HPT150003

A fine home has little to do with the latest trends and lots to do with creating spaces that are livable as well as out-of-this-world beautiful. This graceful Georgian-style home was carefully crafted to blend casual and formal ingredients, and comfortably accommodate a couple with a sophisticated palate for design. No strangers to the realm of residential architecture, Stephen Fuller's parents wanted nothing more than to sink roots in an original design that would suit their lifestyles and convey elements of his signature style.

An elegant front portico, enhanced by four Doric-style columns and a rail with Chippendale detailing, is large enough to greet guests. A fanlight transom tops the paneled entry of this lovely home, and complements keystone arches. The double-door entry opens to an appealing foyer and a formal dining room that offers interior vistas and outdoor views. Nearby, the spacious great room features a coffered ceiling, a fireplace, built-in shelving and French doors that lead to a sun room.

The prevalent use of natural light was a primary objective in creating the design. This bright reprieve begins with the sun room and breakfast nook, which receive a sense of the outdoors through carefully placed skylights. Between these two areas, a set of French doors leads out to a spacious side deck, designed to provide a sense of privacy. A well-planned gourmet kitchen boasts a cooktop island counter and a triple-window view of the front property.

The secluded owners suite, also with deck access, features a tray-ceiling detail in the bedroom and amenities such as a knee-space vanity and walk-in closet in the bath. Family bedrooms, each with a

Above: Wide views enhance the breakfast area.

Top Right: The gourmet kitchen boasts an island counter.

Left: The family room hosts gatherings grand and cozy.

walk-in closet, adjoin a full bath. To the rear of the plan, one of the secondary bedrooms offers the possibility of a home office. A cozy craft room, accessible from the garage, provides a comfortable place to work on home projects.

Right: A simple balustrade lines the staircase that leads to the pool area.

Below: Sitting space in the owners bedroom provides access to the deck.

This home, as shown in the photographs, may differ from the actual blueprints. For more detailed information, please check the floor plans carefully.

Interior design by Stephen Fuller, Inc

DESIGN HPT150003

Square Footage: 2,752 sq. ft.
Width: 80'-0"
Depth: 72'-10"

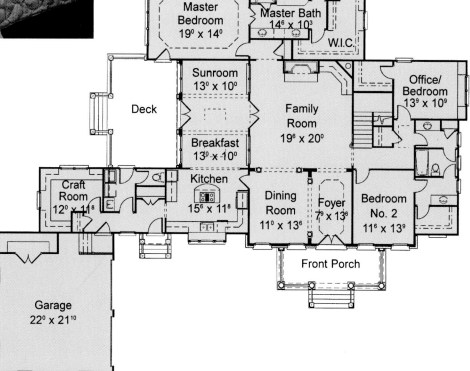

Design by
©Stephen Fuller, Inc.

DESIGN HPT150006

First Floor: 1,387 sq. ft.
Second Floor: 929 sq. ft.
Total: 2,316 sq. ft.
Width: 30'-0"
Depth: 51'-8"

Cost to build? See page 182 to order complete cost estimate to build this house in your area!

Design by
©Home Planners

Perfect for a narrow lot, this shingle-and-stone Nantucket Cape home caters to the casual lifestyle. The side entrance gives direct access to the wonderfully open living areas: the gathering room with a fireplace and an abundance of windows; the island kitchen with an angled, pass-through snack bar; and the dining area with sliding glass doors to a covered eating area. Note also the large deck that further extends the living potential. Also on this floor, the large master bedroom holds a compartmented bath, private dressing room and walk-in closet. Upstairs you'll find the three family bedrooms. Of the two bedrooms with walk-in closets that share a private bath, one features a private balcony.

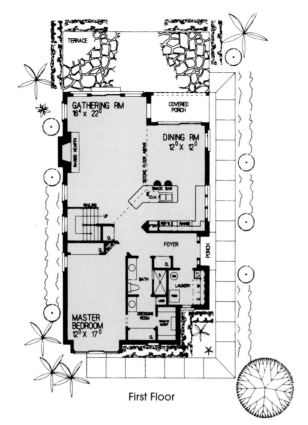

First Floor

Second Floor

Photo by Andy Lautman, Lautman Photography

This home, as shown in the photograph, may differ from the actual blueprints. For more detailed information, please check the floor plans carefully.

Photo courtesy of DLJ Studios

DESIGN HPT150007

First Floor: 2,514 sq. ft.
Second Floor: 975 sq. ft.
Total: 3,489 sq. ft.
Width: 74'-8"
Depth: 64'-8"

Design by
©Ahmann Design, Inc.

You are sure to fall in love with what this French country two-story home has to offer. This four-bedroom, three-car garage home is perfect for the active growing family. Upon arrival, you will be impressed with the two-story entry and beautiful staircase. The great room will capture your attention with its fireplace surrounded by built-in cabinets, two-story ceiling and striking arched windows. The kitchen provides a walk-in pantry, eating bar and island. The nook will welcome you with the rays of light that flow from the skylights in the vaulted ceiling and the view of the backyard. The study will provide you a corner of the house with a view to the front and side. The master bedroom will amaze you with the amount of space that it offers in the room itself and the walk-in closets. The master bath will impress you with a welcoming arch over the bathtub, a large shower and luxurious tub.

First Floor

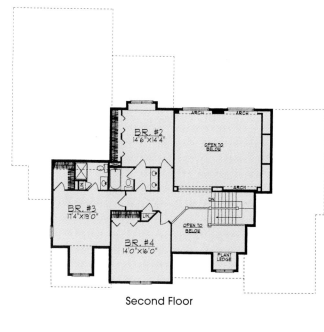

Second Floor

Photo by Riley & Riley Photography, Inc.

This charming country home gives a warm welcome inside and out. Designed for maximum livability, the foyer leads to all areas of the house to minimize corridor space. The dining room begins with round columns at the entrance while the great room boasts a cathedral ceiling, fireplace and arched passage to the large country kitchen. An angled cooktop island and breakfast nook complete the kitchen area. In the master bedroom, there are two walk-in closets, double basins, a lavish bath and separate shower. Two bedrooms and a full bath occupy the second floor. Bonus space over the garage can be developed later.

DESIGN HPT150008

First Floor: 1,416 sq. ft.
Second Floor: 445 sq. ft.
Total: 1,861 sq. ft.
Bonus Room: 284 sq. ft.
Width: 58'-3"
Depth: 68'-9"

Design by
Donald A. Gardner
Architects, Inc.

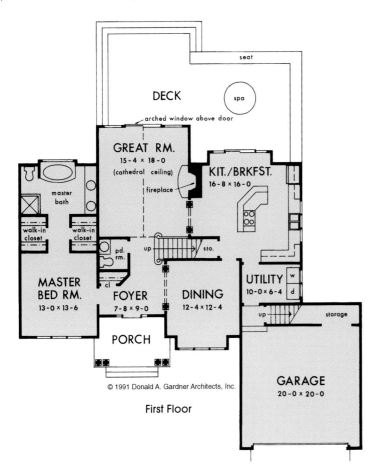

DECK

seat

spa

arched window above door

GREAT RM.
15-4 × 18-0
(cathedral ceiling)

fireplace

KIT./BRKFST.
16-8 × 16-0

master bath

walk-in closet

walk-in closet

pd. rm.

up

sto.

MASTER BED RM.
13-0 × 13-6

cl

FOYER
7-8 × 9-0

DINING
12-4 × 12-4

UTILITY
10-0 × 6-4

w
d

up

storage

PORCH

© 1991 Donald A. Gardner Architects, Inc.

GARAGE
20-0 × 20-0

First Floor

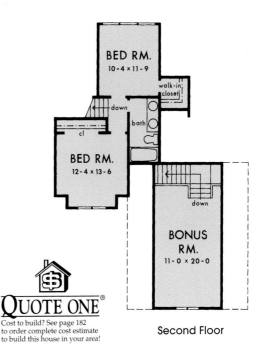

BED RM.
10-4 × 11-9

walk-in closet

down

bath

cl

BED RM.
12-4 × 13-6

down

BONUS RM.
11-0 × 20-0

Second Floor

DESIGN HPT150009

First Floor: 1,661 sq. ft.
Second Floor: 882 sq. ft.
Total: 2,543 sq. ft.
Width: 59'-0"
Depth: 58'-11"

Design by
©Living Concepts
Home Planning

With rustic rafter tails, sturdy pillars and a siding-and-shingle facade, this welcoming bungalow offers plenty of curb appeal. Inside, the formal dining room sits to the left of the foyer and gives easy access to the angled kitchen. A spacious gathering room offers a fireplace, built-ins, a wall of windows and access to a covered terrace. Located on the first floor for privacy, the master bedroom is lavish with its amenities, including His and Hers walk-in closets and basins, a garden tub and a compartmented toilet. Upstairs, two suites offer private baths and share a link retreat that includes a fairway veranda.

First Floor

Second Floor

Photo courtesy of Living Concepts Home Planning

This home, as shown in the photograph, may differ from the actual blueprints.
For more detailed information, please check the floor plans carefully.

A covered porch, multi-pane windows and shingle with stone siding combine to give this bungalow plenty of curb appeal. Inside, the foyer is flanked by the formal living room and an angled staircase. The formal dining room joins the living room, and the kitchen is accessible through double doors. A large family room is graced by a fireplace and opens off a cozy eating nook. The second level presents many attractive angles. The master suite offers a spacious walk-in closet and a sumptuous bath complete with a garden tub and separate shower. Three family bedrooms share a full hall bath.

First Floor: 1,205 sq. ft.
Second Floor: 1,123 sq. ft.
Total: 2,328 sq. ft.
Width: 57'-2"
Depth: 58'-7"

Design by
©Alan Mascord Design Associates, Inc.

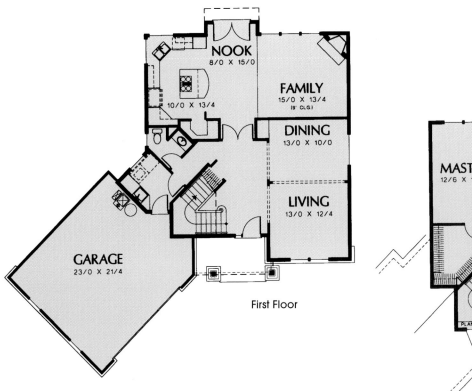

First Floor

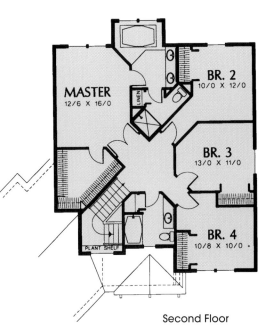

Second Floor

Photo by Bob Greenspan

This home, as shown in the photograph, may differ from the actual blueprints. For more detailed information, please check the floor plans carefully.

Photo courtesy of Stephen Fuller, Inc.

DESIGN HPT150011

First Floor: 1,450 sq. ft.
Second Floor: 1,795 sq. ft.
Total: 3,245 sq. ft.
Width: 61'-5"
Depth: 49'-0"

Design by
©Stephen Fuller, Inc.

Stucco and stone with cedar shingle accents combine to make this country cottage uniquely captivating. The two-story foyer with its unique winding stair opens to the living room and dining room. The family room is the quintessential gathering place and includes a fireplace. A side and rear porch opens both to the family room and the breakfast room, serving as a warm-weather extension of the living space. Up the angled staircase, three spacious bedrooms each offer private bath access. Across the balcony, the dramatic master suite is highlighted by a fireplace and a completely private second-floor porch. The master bath features His and Hers vanities, a garden tub and a generously sized walk-in closet. This home is designed with a walk-out basement foundation.

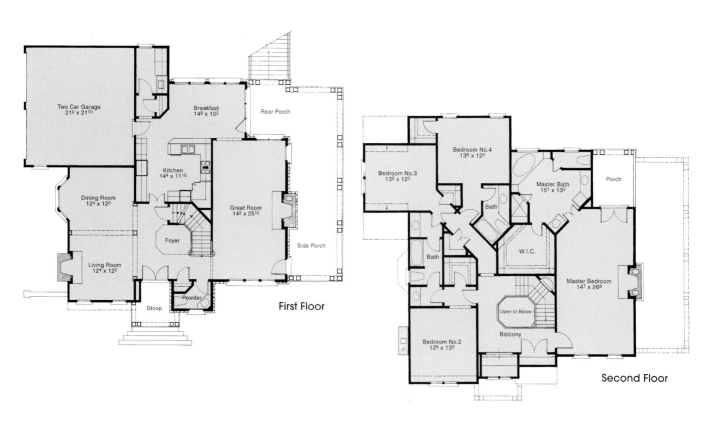

First Floor

Second Floor

Photo courtesy of Stephen Fuller, Inc.

This home is a true Southern original. Inside, the spacious foyer leads directly to a vaulted great room with a handsome fireplace. The dining room, just off the foyer, features a dramatic vaulted ceiling. The kitchen offers both storage and large work areas opening up to the breakfast room. At the rear of the home, you will find the master bedroom with its garden bath, His and Hers vanities and oversized closet. The second floor provides two additional bedrooms with a shared bath and a balcony overlook. Storage space or a fourth bedroom may be placed over the garage area. This home is designed with a walkout basement foundation.

DESIGN HPT150012

First Floor: 1,944 sq. ft.
Second Floor: 1,055 sq. ft.
Total: 2,999 sq. ft.
Width: 51'-6"
Depth: 72'-0"

Design by
©Stephen Fuller, Inc.

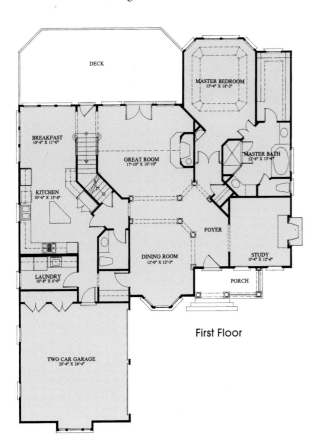

First Floor

Second Floor

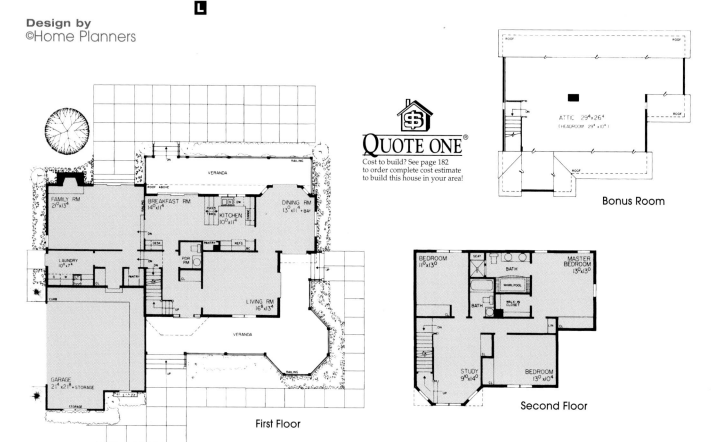

Photo by Andrew D. Lautman

DESIGN HPT150013

First Floor: 1,375 sq. ft.
Second Floor: 1,016 sq. ft.
Total: 2,391 sq. ft.
Bonus Room: 303 sq. ft.
Width: 62'-7"
Depth: 54'-0"

L

Design by
©Home Planners

Covered porches, front and back, are a fine preview to the livable nature of this Victorian design. Living areas are defined by a family room with a fireplace, formal living and dining rooms and a kitchen with a breakfast room. An ample laundry room, a garage with a storage area and a powder room round out the first floor. Three second-floor bedrooms are joined by a study and two full baths. The master bedroom on this floor boasts two closets, including an ample walk-in, as well as a relaxing bath with a tile-rimmed whirlpool tub and a separate shower with a seat.

QUOTE ONE®
Cost to build? See page 182
to order complete cost estimate
to build this house in your area!

Bonus Room

ATTIC 29⁴x26⁴
(HEADROOM 29⁴x10⁴)

First Floor

VERANDA
RAILING
FAMILY RM
21⁰x13⁴
BREAKFAST RM
14⁰x11⁴
DINING RM
13⁰x11⁴ + BAY
KITCHEN
10⁰x11⁴
LAUNDRY
10⁰x7⁴
PANTRY
PDR RM
LIVING RM
16⁸x13⁴
VERANDA
GARAGE
21⁴x21⁸ + STORAGE
STORAGE
RAILING

Second Floor

BEDROOM
11⁰x13⁰
SEAT
BATH
MASTER BEDROOM
13⁰x13⁰
WHIRL POOL
BATH
WALK-IN CLOSET
STUDY
9¹⁰x14⁰
BEDROOM
13⁰x10⁴

New England Classics

*Cape Cod, Nantucket Island
and Colonial Designs*

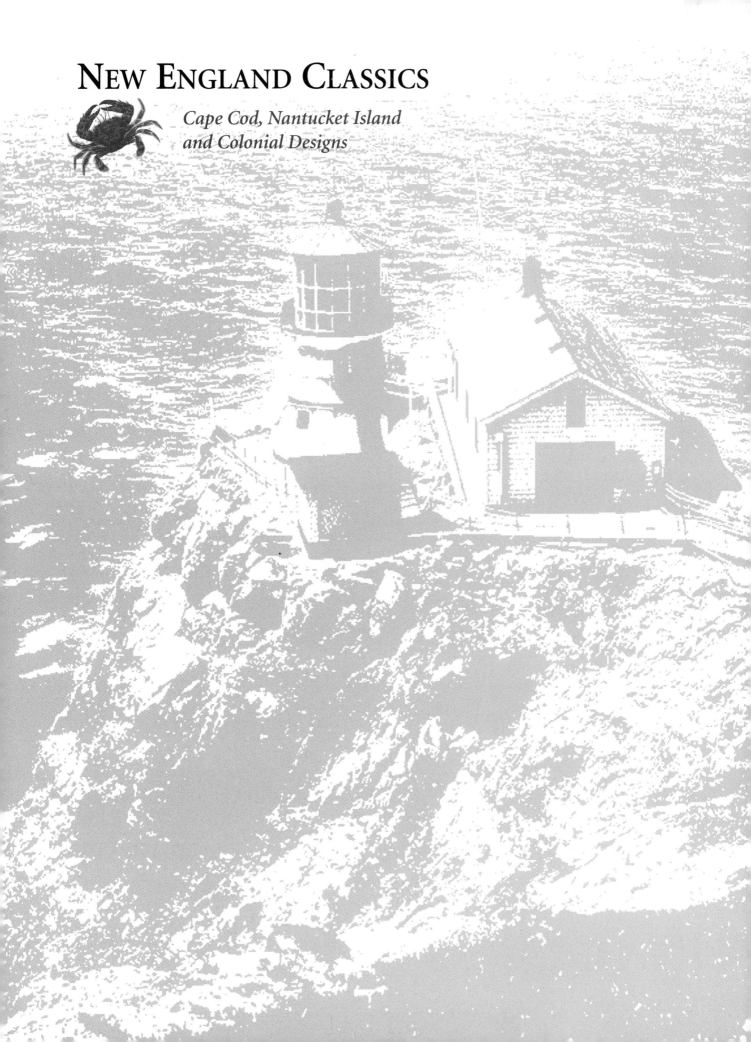

DESIGN HPT150014

First Floor: 1,567 sq. ft.
Second Floor: 1,895 sq. ft.
Total: 3,462 sq. ft.
Width: 63'-0"
Depth: 53'-6"

Although the facade may look like a quaint country cottage, this home's fine proportions contain formal living areas, including a dining room and a living room. At the back of the first floor, you'll find a spacious kitchen and a breakfast nook. The great room, with a fireplace and a bumped-out window, makes everyday living very comfortable. A rear porch allows for outdoor dining and relaxation. Upstairs, four bedrooms include a master bedroom with lots of notable features. A boxed ceiling, lavish bath, large walk-in closet and secluded sitting room—which would also make a nice study or exercise room—assure great livability. One of the family bedrooms contains a full bath. This home is designed with a walkout basement foundation.

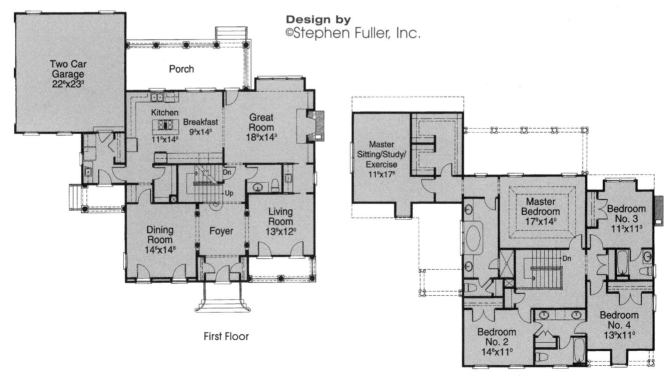

Design by
©Stephen Fuller, Inc.

First Floor

Second Floor

This stately plan, ideal for a narrow lot, is adorned with an eyebrow dormer, French-style shutters and fine brick detailing. The porch leads into a long foyer, flanked on the right by a dining room and on the left by a study. A long, narrow porch dominates the right side of the plan. The great room is at the rear of the plan, away from the noise of traffic, and boasts a fireplace and access to the porch. The kitchen leads to a bayed breakfast area, which looks out to the side porch. The second level is home to the master bedroom—full bath included—and two family bedrooms, which share a walk-through full bath. A loft and a full bath grace the third level.

DESIGN HPT150015

First Floor: 1,590 sq. ft.
Second Floor: 1,525 sq. ft.
Third Floor: 500 sq. ft.
Total: 3,615 sq. ft.
Width: 36'-0"
Depth: 58'-4"

Design by
©Garden Houses
of the 1920s, LLC

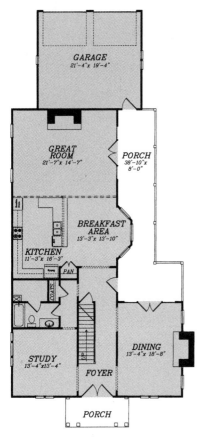

First Floor

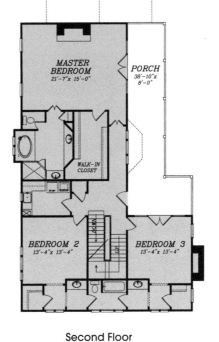

Second Floor

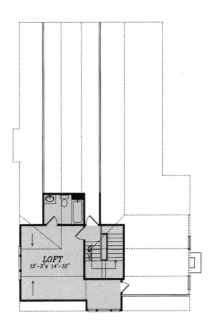

Third Floor

SHINGLE STYLE

DESIGN HPT150016

First Floor: 1,317 sq. ft.
Second Floor: 681 sq. ft.
Total: 1,998 sq. ft.
Width: 59'-8"
Depth: 37'-8"

This Cape Cod-style house combines the sloped rear roof, tall front facade and shingled exterior of a traditional Nantucket cottage. Based on the 1763 Edward Allen House, random-width wood paneling, exposed beams in the keeping room and a simple balustrade along the curving staircase add rustic appeal to the interior. The large center chimney supports fireplaces in the keeping and living rooms. As its Colonial predecessors, this plan places the kitchen in the lean-to section of the house. The U-shaped work area includes a pass-through to the eating area. A first-floor bedroom could also function well as a study or a home office. Plenty of storage space is available in two upstairs bedrooms sharing a full bath.

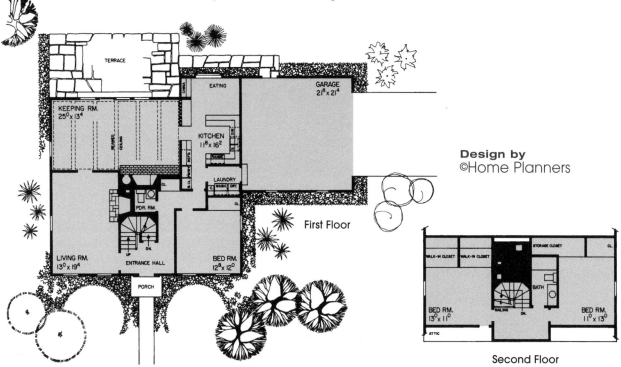

First Floor

Design by
©Home Planners

Second Floor

This version of a Nantucket Island saltbox is adapted from a cottage built around 1820 by Captain Alexander Bunker. The exterior includes many of the details of the original, including the shuttered front door and the classic entablature over the front doorway. Although the garage is a modern addition, the location of the kitchen—in the attached lean-to at the back of the house—is the same. The kitchen itself is totally up-to-date, with spaces for today's appliances and a large U-shaped work area. Down a step from the main hall, the kitchen offers sliding glass doors to a flagstone-paved terrace, as does the nearby dining room. The living room with a fireplace, a family bedroom and the laundry room complete the first floor. Upstairs, the master bedroom offers a large walk-in closet and a separate vanity area in a bath shared with a third bedroom.

DESIGN HPT150017

First Floor: 1,211 sq. ft.
Second Floor: 747 sq. ft.
Total: 1,958 sq. ft.
Width: 52'-0"
Depth: 48'-0"

Design by
©Home Planners

Second Floor

First Floor

DESIGN HPT150018

First Floor: 1,385 sq. ft.
Second Floor: 982 sq. ft.
Total: 2,367 sq. ft.
Width: 63'-8"
Depth: 46'-0"

This cozy three-bedroom Cape Cod design draws its inspiration from the Joseph Atwood House, the oldest house in Chatham, Massachusetts. It was built in 1752 by a sea captain who made long voyages to all parts of the globe. A century later it was the home of Joseph C. Lincoln, author of stories about Cape Cod. Although Capes usually had single-pitch roofs, the builder of the Atwood House used the gambrel roof to increase the amount of headroom on the second floor. Updated floor plans give this full-size cottage a large country kitchen with a bay window and a work island/snack bar. Formal living and dining rooms sit across the front of the house. The ell holds a mudroom with a pantry and a washroom, a laundry room and a garage. Three bedrooms reside upstairs, including a master suite with a deluxe bath.

Design by
©Home Planners

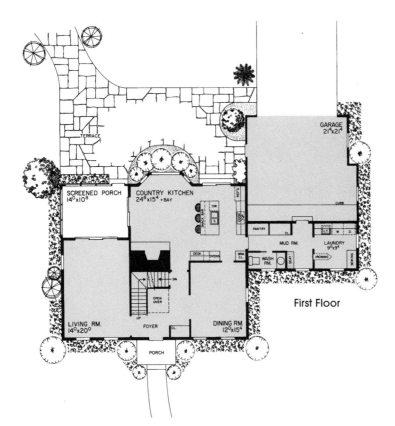

First Floor

Second Floor

The his Colonial home possesses all the exterior charm of its Early American ancestors—paired windows flank the entry while shed dormers add headroom to the second story. A modern interior makes it perfect for today. To the immediate left of the entry is a living room with a music alcove and a fireplace. To the right is the formal dining room. A few steps down from the living room, a cheery sun room sits in its own wing. The country kitchen, with an island cooktop, built-in china cabinets and a fireplace, offers plenty of space for informal eating. Both it and the music alcove have sliding doors to the rear terrace. A spacious laundry room and a washroom complete this level. Upstairs, two family bedrooms share a full bath, while the master suite pampers with a whirlpool tub, twin vanities and plenty of closet space.

DESIGN HPT150019

First Floor: 1,592 sq. ft.
Second Floor: 1,054 sq. ft.
Total: 2,646 sq. ft.
Width: 64'-0"
Depth: 48'-8"

Design by
©Home Planners

Cost to build? See page 182
to order complete cost estimate
to build this house in your area!

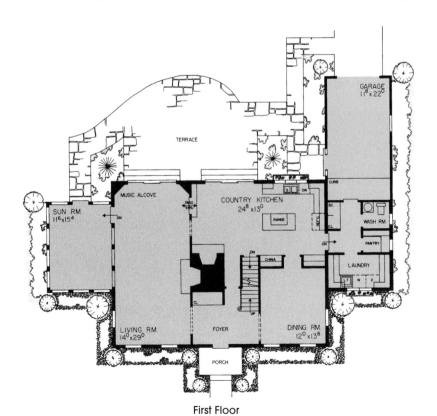

First Floor

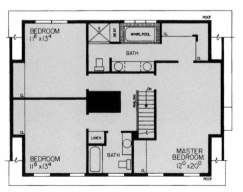

Second Floor

SHINGLE STYLE

DESIGN HPT150020

First Floor: 1,389 sq. ft.
Second Floor: 1,049 sq. ft.
Total: 2,438 sq. ft.
Width: 45'-0"
Depth: 51'-0"

Design by
©Alan Mascord Design
Associates, Inc.

Shingles, stonework and skylights all combine to make this country house a delight in which to live. The pleasure continues inside with a two-story great room acting as the heart of the home. Here a built-in media center flanks a warming fireplace. The L-shaped island kitchen offers an adjacent bayed nook for casual times, while the formal dining room easily accommodates elegant dinner parties. A den with a window seat finishes out the first floor. Nicely open to the first floor, the second floor contains two family bedrooms and a lavish, vaulted master suite. Here, reach a walk-in closet via a luxurious bath that includes twin vanities and a separate shower and tub.

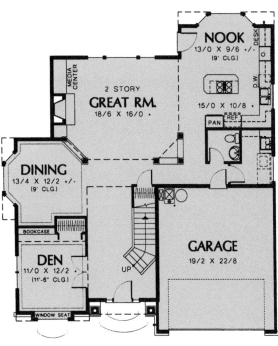

First Floor

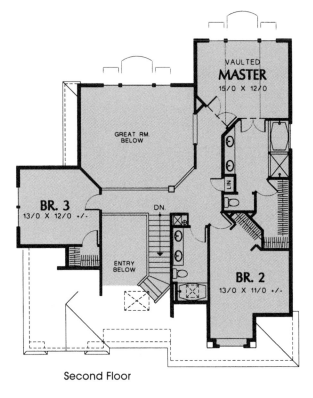

Second Floor

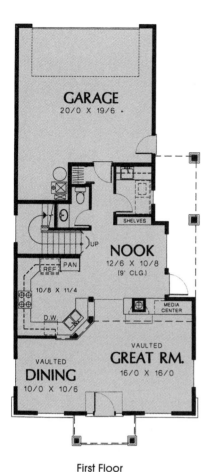

GARAGE
20/0 X 19/6 +

NOOK
12/6 X 10/8
(9' CLG.)

UP

SHELVES

REF PAN

10/8 X 11/4

D.W

MEDIA CENTER

VAULTED
GREAT RM.
16/0 X 16/0

VAULTED
DINING
10/0 X 10/6

First Floor

Design by
©Alan Mascord Design Associates, Inc.

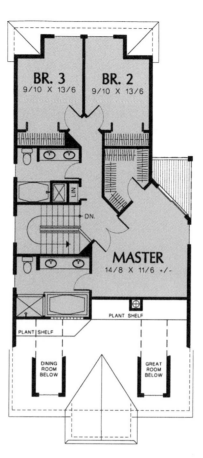

BR. 3
9/10 X 13/6

BR. 2
9/10 X 13/6

LIN

DN.

MASTER
14/8 X 11/6 +/-

PLANT SHELF

PLANT SHELF

DINING ROOM BELOW

GREAT ROOM BELOW

Second Floor

Design HPT150021

First Floor: 847 sq. ft.
Second Floor: 845 sq. ft.
Total: 1,692 sq. ft.
Width: 27'-0"
Depth: 61'-0"

Shingles-and-stone, gables and a covered porch—all elements of Craftsman styling. This petite bungalow is perfect for narrow lots and still provides plenty of amenities for the whole family. The entry opens directly into the vaulted great room. Here, a wood stove, built-ins and an adjacent, vaulted dining room provide fantastic ambiance. The C-shaped kitchen features a sink overlooking the great room, a pantry and plenty of counter and cabinet space. A nearby nook offers outdoor access and built-in shelves. Upstairs, the master suite is designed to pamper with a private balcony, walk-in closet and pampering bath. Two secondary bedrooms share a full hall bath that includes a dual-bowl vanity. The two-car garage enters from the back of the property, hiding it effectively from the road.

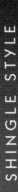

DESIGN HPT150022

First Floor: 1,229 sq. ft.
Second Floor: 551 sq. ft.
Total: 1,780 sq. ft.
Width: 63'-0"
Depth: 32'-0"

The recessed entry of this 1½-story, three-bedroom Cape Cod design opens to a large family room with a fireplace and pass-through window to the island kitchen. The dining room accesses the rear deck and is situated conveniently near the kitchen. The secluded master suite is complete with a large walk-in closet, twin vanity sinks and separate shower and tub. Upstairs, two family bedrooms enjoy dormer windows, ample closet space, one full bath and access to lots of attic storage for all the family treasures.

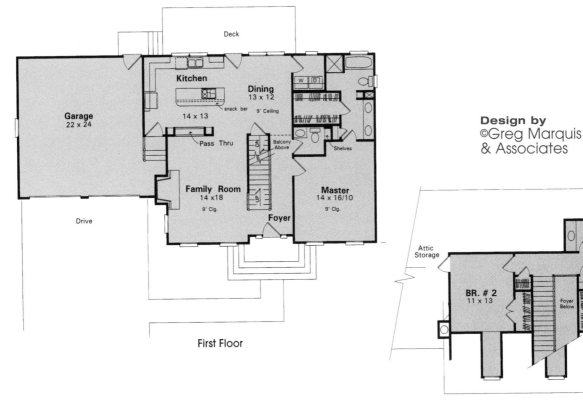

Design by
©Greg Marquis
& Associates

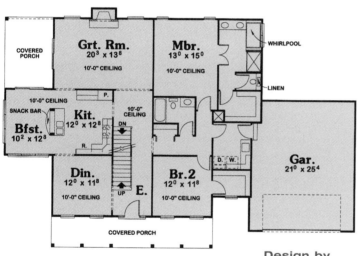

DESIGN HPT150023

Square Footage: 1,768
Bonus Space: 841 sq. ft.
Width: 72'-8"
Depth: 42'-0"

Design by
©Design Basics, Inc.

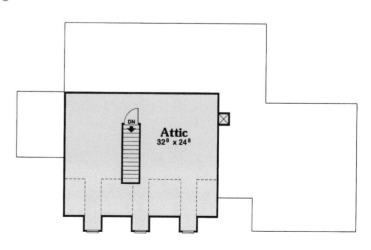

Three gabled dormers and an array of arches on a covered porch welcome every family member or guest into a comfortable two-bedroom home. The formal dining room directly off the right side of the foyer leads into a pleasing kitchen with a snack bar and breakfast nook. Located just behind the kitchen, the great room includes a hearth and sliding doors accessible to the rear covered porch. Inside the master bedroom, a private bath caters to His and Hers needs with a double-sink vanity, garden tub and separate shower. The additional bedroom across the way contains a huge walk-in closet. Also nearby is the second full bath and hall closet. Notice a roomy utility room and the two-car garage.

Master Bath

w.i.c.

Covered Patio

Master Bedroom
18⁰ · 16⁰

Family
22⁰ · 15⁰

Dining
12⁰ · 11⁴

Kitchen

Library
14⁰ · 12⁰

Nook

Foyer

Bath

Entry

Utility

2 Car Garage

First Floor

I nteresting rooflines, dormers, French-style shutters and a country cupola complete the exterior of this plan. The foyer leads to a library with built-in bookshelves, perfect for quiet reading. The hearth-warmed family room flows into the dining room, which easily accesses the kitchen and bayed breakfast nook. The island kitchen is graced with plentiful counter space and access to a half-bath and utility room. The first-floor master suite is located at the rear of the plan for increased privacy, and includes a walk-in closet, access to a covered patio and a full bath. Two family bedrooms reside upstairs; both have ample closet space and share a hall bath. Unfinished storage and expandable space complete this floor.

Bedroom 2
16⁰ · 13⁰

closet

Unfinished Storage
14⁴ · 14⁴

closet

down

Bath

Bedroom 3
13⁰ · 11⁰

Desk

Linen

Mech.

stor.

Expand. Space
12⁰ · 24⁰

Design by
©Home Design Services, Inc.

Second Floor

DESIGN HPT150024

First Floor: 1,889 sq. ft.
Second Floor: 798 sq. ft.
Total: 2,687 sq. ft.
Bonus Room: 356 sq. ft.
Width: 38'-8"
Depth: 95'-0"

ultiple dormers, a charming cupola and a prominent bay window give this home great curb appeal. The entry is flanked on the right by a dining room, complete with a tray ceiling and a bay window looking to the front property. Just off the foyer, the family room boasts a fireplace and a vaulted ceiling. The right side of the first floor is devoted mainly to the kitchen, nook and laundry area. Also on this floor, a convenient porte cochere leads from the laundry room to the two-car garage, perfect for stormy weather. A master bedroom, complete with a full bath and walk-in closet, finishes this floor. The second level is home to two additional bedrooms, one future bedroom and space for a future bonus room.

DESIGN HPT150025

First Floor: 1,530 sq. ft.
Second Floor: 777 sq. ft.
Total: 2,307 sq. ft.
Bonus Room: 361 sq. ft.
Width: 61'-4"
Depth: 78'-0"

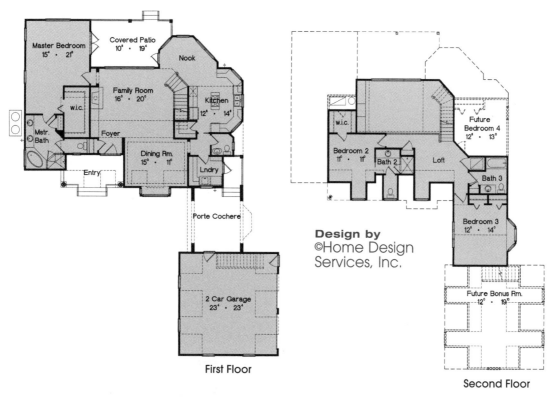

Design by
©Home Design
Services, Inc.

First Floor

Second Floor

DESIGN HPT150026

First Floor: 1,326 sq. ft.
Second Floor: 1,254 sq. ft.
Total: 2,580 sq. ft.
Width: 55'-4"
Depth: 57'-6"

This shingle-style home is a rustic, yet elegant design that does not reveal itself fully at first glance. Double French doors at the entrance lead to a magnificent gallery hall and winding staircase. Stunning columns define the formal dining room, while French doors open to the front porch. The central hall leads to a quiet study and to the octagonal great room, which offers a fireplace, built-in bookshelves and access to the rear deck. A spacious kitchen opens to the breakfast room that features a service entrance from the one-car garage. The dramatic staircase outside the great room leads upstairs, where a charming master bedroom includes a fireplace, walk-in closet and two vanities. This home is designed with a basement foundation.

Design by
©Stephen Fuller, Inc.

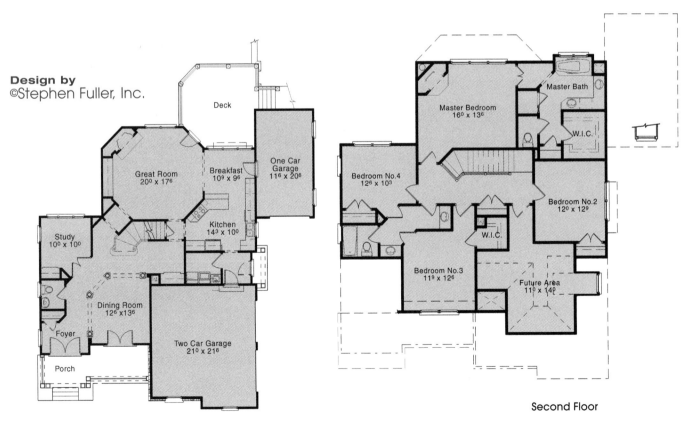

First Floor

Second Floor

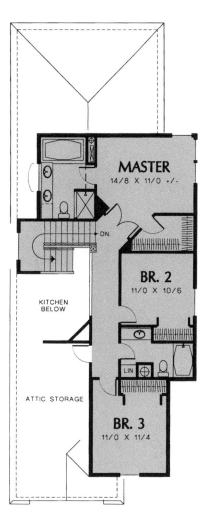

Design by
©Alan Mascord Design
Associates, Inc.

First Floor

GARAGE
20/0 X 20/6

NOOK
14/6 X 9/4
(9' CLG.)

UP

PAN

VAULTED
KIT
11/0 X 10/0

REF

FAMILY RM.
15/2 X 12/2 +/-
(9' CLG.)

MEDIA
CENTER

DINING
11/0 X 10/0
(9' CLG.)

LIVING RM.
14/0 X 12/0
(9' CLG.)

First Floor

MASTER
14/8 X 11/0 +/-

DN.

BR. 2
11/0 X 10/6

KITCHEN
BELOW

LIN

ATTIC STORAGE

BR. 3
11/0 X 11/4

Second Floor

DESIGN HPT150027

First Floor: 1,027 sq. ft.
Second Floor: 849 sq. ft.
Total: 1,876 sq. ft.
Width: 27'-0"
Depth: 68'-0"

Shingles, siding and stone, plus many other attractive details, combine to create a wonderful look for this narrow-lot, three-bedroom home. Inside, the foyer opens directly to the living area, starting at the formal dining room directly ahead and flanked by the formal living room to the left and the spacious family room—complete with a fireplace and built-in media center—to the right. The U-shaped, vaulted kitchen offers a snack bar into the family room, and works well with the nearby nook. Upstairs, a balcony overlooks the kitchen and leads to two family bedrooms sharing a full bath. The master bedroom is sure to please, with a walk-in closet and a lavish bath.

DESIGN HPT150028

First Floor: 1,886 sq. ft.
Second Floor: 2,076 sq. ft.
Total: 3,962 sq. ft.
Width: 49'-0"
Depth: 75'-0"

This handsome design has a heart of gold: a gourmet kitchen and an open living area with a morning nook and two sets of French doors to the rear deck. A spacious guest bedroom leads to the side porch. The dramatic front hall leads to a flex room and a formal dining room, then to a large great room. Upstairs, the master suite is a spacious retreat, complete with a private study or sitting room. A second-floor guest suite provides its own access to the morning nook and kitchen via a rear staircase. This home is designed with a basement foundation.

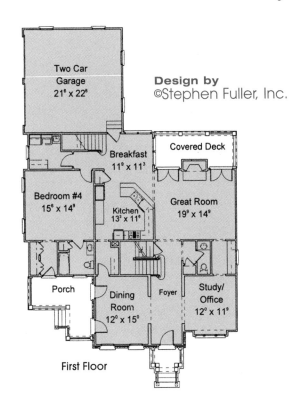

Design by
©Stephen Fuller, Inc.

Two Car Garage
21⁶ x 22⁶

Breakfast
11⁹ x 11³

Covered Deck

Bedroom #4
15⁶ x 14⁹

Kitchen
13³ x 11⁹

Great Room
19⁹ x 14⁹

Porch

Dining Room
12⁰ x 15⁰

Foyer

Study/ Office
12⁰ x 11⁹

First Floor

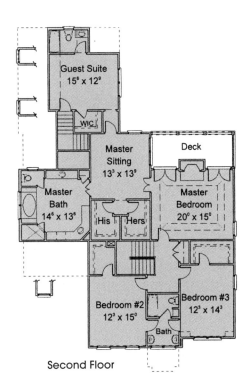

Guest Suite
15⁶ x 12⁹

WIC

Master Sitting
13³ x 13⁹

Deck

Master Bath
14⁶ x 13⁹

His   Hers

Master Bedroom
20⁰ x 15⁰

Bedroom #2
12³ x 15⁰

Bedroom #3
12³ x 14³

Bath

Second Floor

A symmetrical gables, double columns and a gabled entrance add visual interest to this charming exterior. Inside, the wraparound main hall opens to the formal rooms and casual living space—an inviting arrangement for entertaining. The living room, with a bumped-out bay window, adjoins the dining room. The U-shaped kitchen features an island work counter and ample cabinet and counter space. The comfortable family room provides built-in bookshelves and a large hearth. The master suite includes a spacious bath, and two closets provide plenty of wardrobe space. Upstairs, Bedroom 4, with a private bath and abundant closet space, would work well as a guest suite. Bedrooms 2 and 3 share a full bath, and a study area adjoins Bedroom 2. An additional storage closet is provided in the two-car garage. This home is designed with a basement foundation.

DESIGN HPT150029

First Floor: 2,012 sq. ft.
Second Floor: 1,254 sq. ft.
Total: 3,266 sq. ft.
Width: 70'-0"
Depth: 75'-6"

Design by
©Stephen Fuller, Inc.

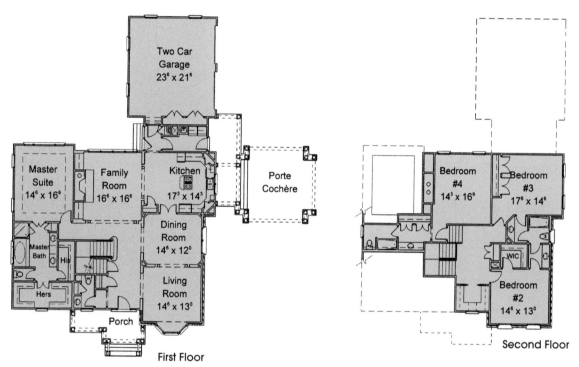

DESIGN HPT150030

First Floor: 1,840 sq. ft.
Second Floor: 957 sq. ft.
Total: 2,797 sq. ft.
Width: 72'-0"
Depth: 72'-6"

In addition to an attached two-car garage, this Cape Cod design features a covered car entry for rainy days. The foyer opens to a large family room with a fireplace and a pass-through window to the island kitchen. Great views of the front yard are possible through the dining room's box-bay window. The master suite—which boasts His and Hers walk-in closets and basins, a compartmented toilet and separate shower and tub—dwells on the first floor, while two family bedrooms, a full bath and lots of attic storage occupies the second floor. This home is designed with a basement foundation.

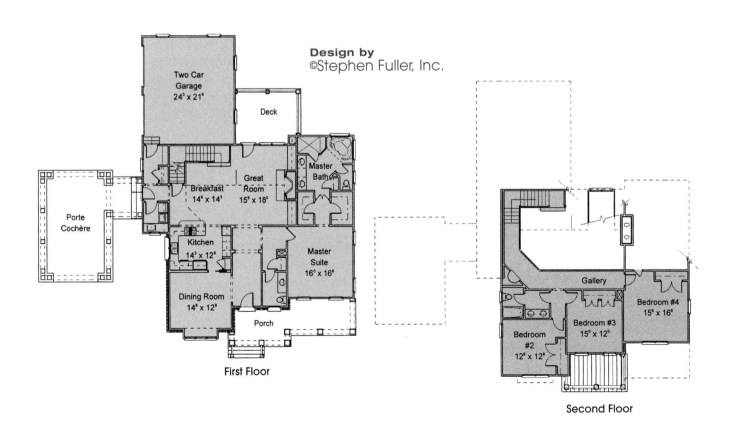

Design by
©Stephen Fuller, Inc.

Two Car Garage 24³ x 21⁶

Deck

Porte Cochère

Breakfast 14⁴ x 14³

Great Room 15⁹ x 18⁰

Master Bath

Kitchen 14³ x 12⁹

Master Suite 16⁰ x 16⁰

Dining Room 14⁴ x 12⁹

Porch

First Floor

Gallery

Bedroom #4 15⁶ x 16⁶

Bedroom #3 15⁶ x 12⁰

Bedroom #2 12⁶ x 12⁰

Second Floor

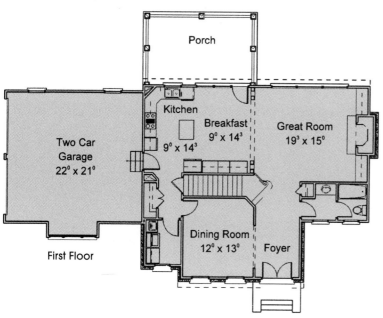

Porch

Kitchen

Breakfast
9⁰ x 14³

Great Room
19³ x 15⁰

Two Car
Garage
22⁰ x 21⁰

Dining Room
12⁰ x 13⁰

Foyer

First Floor

This beautiful home features an overhanging second floor with dramatic drop pendants. Inside, the foyer shows gorgeous interior vistas past the staircase to the open great room, which sports a fireplace and plenty of windows for pleasant backyard views. A gourmet kitchen adjoins the breakfast nook, with access to the rear porch. Upstairs, the master suite provides lovely views to the backyard and includes a walk-in closet and a full bath with two basins and a separate shower and tub. Two additional bedrooms, a study alcove and a bonus room provide additional space. This home is designed with a basement foundation.

DESIGN HPT150031

First Floor: 1,104 sq. ft.
Second Floor: 1,144 sq. ft.
Total: 2,248 sq. ft.
Bonus Room: 242 sq. ft.
Width: 62'-6"
Depth: 32'-0"

Design by
©Stephen Fuller, Inc.

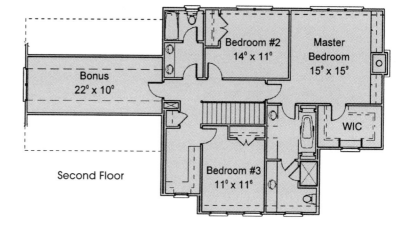

Bonus
22⁰ x 10⁰

Bedroom #2
14⁰ x 11⁰

Master
Bedroom
15⁹ x 15⁹

WIC

Bedroom #3
11⁰ x 11⁶

Second Floor

Photo courtesy of Living Concepts Home Planning

DESIGN HPT150032

First Floor: 2,538 sq. ft.
Second Floor: 1,581 sq. ft.
Total: 4,119 sq. ft.
Bonus Space: 1,773 sq. ft.
Width: 67'-7"
Depth: 84'-5"

Double columns flank the grand portico of this fine two-story home. Inside, the foyer presents a formal living room. This room welcomes all with a beam ceiling and a wall of windows to the rear veranda. The C-shaped kitchen offers a work-surface island, a walk-in pantry and easy access to the spacious gathering room. Located on the first floor for privacy, the master suite is lavish with its luxuries. Upstairs, two family suites—each with a walk-in closet—share a full bath, while the large guest suite features another walk-in closet as well as a private bath.

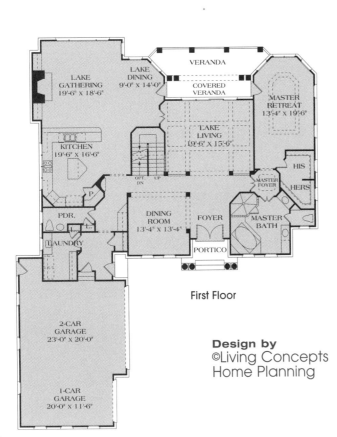

First Floor

Second Floor

Design by
©Living Concepts
Home Planning

CRAFTSMAN CHARACTER

Craftsman and bungalow homes

DESIGN HPT150033

First Floor: 2,918 sq. ft.
Second Floor: 330 sq. ft.
Total: 3,248 sq. ft.
Width: 82'-8"
Depth: 60'-0"

Design by
©Home Planners

L

Verandas at both the front and rear of this engaging bungalow provide outdoor enthusiasts with a front-row seat to enjoy the changing seasons. To further entice you outdoors, the master bedroom, the breakfast room and the gathering room all have French doors that open to the rear veranda. During frosty weather, a raised-hearth fireplace warms the combined gathering room and dining room and offers a friendly invitation. Bedrooms are efficiently separated from the living area. A romantic fireplace and a luxurious private bath enhance the master bedroom. Two family bedrooms share a full bath. The second floor holds a lounge that makes a great getaway for quiet contemplation or study.

QUOTE ONE®
Cost to build? See page 182
to order complete cost estimate
to build this house in your area!

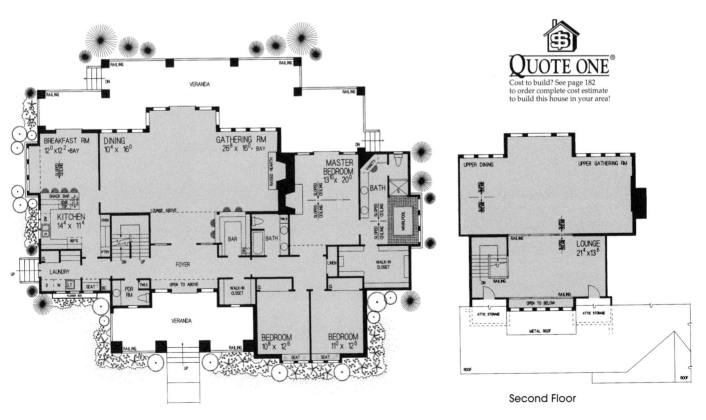

First Floor

Second Floor

Cozy living abounds in this comfortable two-story bungalow. Enter the foyer and find a spacious living room with a fireplace to the left. Straight ahead is a U-shaped kitchen with a snack bar, planning desk and easy access to the formal dining room. The bayed family room features a fireplace and entry to a screened porch. Upstairs secondary bedrooms offer ample closet space and direct access to a shared bath. The master bedroom contains a large walk-in closet, double-bowl vanity and compartmented shower and toilet.

DESIGN HPT150034

First Floor: 1,482 sq. ft.
Second Floor: 885 sq. ft.
Total: 2,367 sq. ft.
Width: 64'-0"
Depth: 50'-0"

L

Design by
©Home Planners

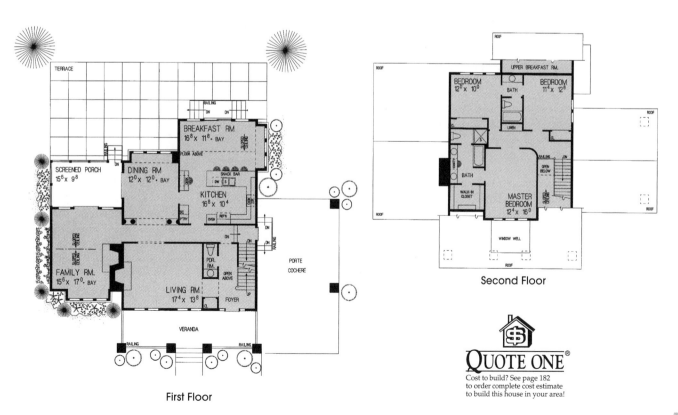

First Floor

Second Floor

DESIGN HPT150035

Main Level: 1,416 sq. ft.
Lower Level: 1,300 sq. ft.
Total: 2,716 sq. ft.
Width: 50'-0"
Depth: 46'-0"

Design by
©Northwest Home
Designing, Inc.

Two gables, supported by pillars and accented with rafter tails, are fine examples of Craftsmanship on this three-bedroom home. Inside, a den opens to the left of the foyer, providing a quiet place for reading. Down a few steps, one comes to the rest of the main-floor living space. A living room with a fireplace flanked by windows welcomes casual times. The unique kitchen offers a small, yet cozy, nook as well as ease in serving the dining room. The master suite is also on this floor and features a walk-in closet and a pampering bath. Downstairs, a huge rec room is available for many pursuits. Two secondary bedrooms share a bath and access to the rear patio also.

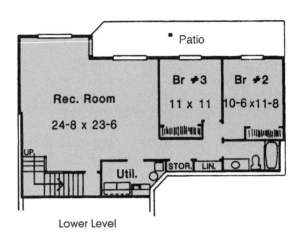

Lower Level

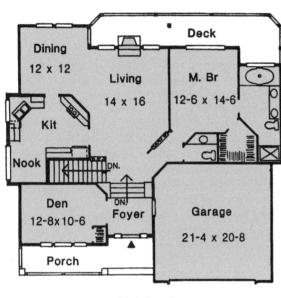

Main Level

3 Car Garage
33'-4" x 20'-8"

Optional

Craftsman style is very evident on this fine bungalow home. From its shingles, gabled rooflines, detailed windows and definitive pillars to its grand layout, this home is sure to please. A spacious great room features a fireplace flanked by windows, a wall of built-ins and easy access to the L-shaped kitchen. Adjacent to the kitchen is a sunny eating area, perfect for early morning coffee. In the sleeping zone, two family bedrooms share a full hall bath, while the master suite is full of amenities. Complete with a walk-in closet, a wall of windows and a sumptuous bath, this suite will be a haven for any homeowner. A loft/bonus area overlooks the great room and offers a private outdoor balcony.

DESIGN HPT150036

Square Footage: 1,941
Bonus Room: 200 sq. ft.
Width: 60'-0"
Depth: 62'-0"

Design by
©Northwest Home
Designing, Inc.

Eating
11 x 9

Deck

M. Br
17 x 12-6

Great Rm.
23 x 16-6

Kitchen

BOOKS TV/ST BOOKS

LIN.

UP

Util./Mud

DN.

Entry

Br #2
11-9 x 12

Br #3
11-9 x 12

Garage
23-4 x 29-8

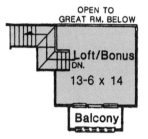

OPEN TO
GREAT RM. BELOW

Loft/Bonus
DN.
13-6 x 14

Balcony

DESIGN HPT150037

First Floor: 1,454 sq. ft.
Second Floor: 627 sq. ft.
Total: 2,081 sq. ft.
Width: 46'-0"
Depth: 52'-0"

Design by
©Northwest Home
Designing, Inc.

Craftsman style is recognized from its various elements, and this bungalow certainly has them. From the pillars at the front door, and the gabled rooflines, to the rafter tails and shingles, this home is sure to be a favorite in any neighborhood. The entryway presents a formal yet cozy parlor, then leads back to the spacious family room. Here, a corner fireplace casts its cheer throughout the room and into the kitchen, where a snack bar does double duty as a work island. A patio is available nearby for dining alfresco. Two bedrooms complete this floor, one a pampering master suite with a walk-in closet and a private bath. Upstairs, a huge rec room is available for more casual pursuits, with a fourth bedroom and a full bath nearby.

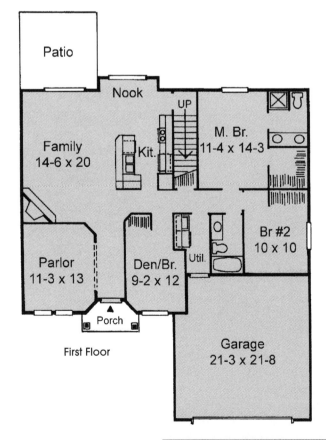

Patio

Nook

UP

Family
14-6 x 20

Kit.

M. Br.
11-4 x 14-3

Parlor
11-3 x 13

Den/Br.
9-2 x 12

Util.

Br #2
10 x 10

Porch

Garage
21-3 x 21-8

First Floor

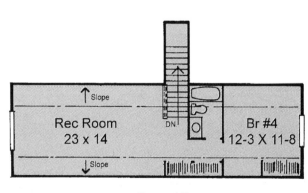

Slope

Rec Room
23 x 14

DN

Br #4
12-3 X 11-8

Slope

Second Floor

Formal living areas in this plan are joined by a three-bedroom sleeping wing. One bedroom, with foyer access, could function as a study. Two verandas and a screened porch enlarge the plan and enhance indoor/outdoor livability. Notice the added extras: the abundant storage space, walk-in pantry, built-in planning desk, whirlpool tub and pass-through snack bar. The sloped ceiling in the gathering room gives this area an open, airy quality. The breakfast room, with its wealth of windows, will be a cheerful and bright space to enjoy a cup of morning coffee.

DESIGN HPT150038

Square Footage: 1,959
Width: 56'-0"
Depth: 48'-8"

L

Design by
©Home Planners

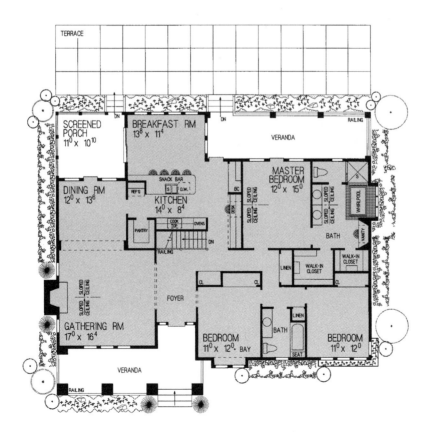

QUOTE ONE®
Cost to build? See page 182
to order complete cost estimate
to build this house in your area!

MASTER
BEDRM
12⁸ × 16⁴

COVERED PATIO

FAMILY
17⁸ × 14⁶

SLOPED CEILING

SLOPED CEILING

DINING
12⁰ × 15⁰

SLOPED CEILING

SNACK BAR

KITCHEN
17² × 12⁰

WIC

DESK

RANGE

M BATH

LIN

VETBAR

PANT

REFG

SHELF

GARDEN TUB

SLOPED CEILING

DN

W D

BATH

LIVING
17⁶ × 14²

RAISED HEARTH

RAILING

BEDRM
10² × 10⁶

BEDRM
11⁶ × 12⁰

SLOPED CEILING

COVERED PORCH

RAILING

DESIGN HPT150039

Square Footage: 2,033
Width: 47'-6"
Depth: 61'-6"

L

Design by
©Home Planners

Get more out of your home-building dollars with this unique one-story bungalow. A covered front porch provides sheltered entry into a spacious living room where a raised hearth and a column are special touches. The dining room enjoys a sloped ceiling, a wet bar and direct access to the rear covered patio. In the nearby kitchen, a breakfast bar accommodates quick meals. The adjacent family room rounds out this casual living area. The large master bedroom pampers with a sitting area, patio access and a luxurious bath that features a corner tub, separate shower and dual lavatories. Two secondary bedrooms share a full hall bath.

QUOTE ONE®

Cost to build? See page 182
to order complete cost estimate
to build this house in your area!

This handsome bungalow is designed for easy living with a floor plan that puts comfort first. Quaint living and dining rooms are separated with a half-wall of built-in shelves. The large kitchen provides an open wet bar to the dining room and a snack bar to the combination breakfast/family room. The extra-large family room has sliding glass doors off the breakfast area and a door opening to the covered rear porch. The master bedroom offers privacy and convenience thanks to thoughtful first-floor planning. The two spacious bedrooms upstairs share a twin-basin bath.

DESIGN HPT150040

First Floor: 1,581 sq. ft.
Second Floor: 592 sq. ft.
Total: 2,173 sq. ft.
Width: 35'-4"
Depth: 66'-0"

Design by
©Home Planners

COVERED PORCH

MASTER
BEDRM
13⁴ x 18⁰

FAMILY
ROOM
15⁴ x 11⁶

MASTER
BATH

BREAKFAST ROOM
15⁴ x 11⁸

DESK

KIT
13⁰ x 11⁴

WET
BAR

DINING
RM
13⁴ x 11⁰

5' HIGH SHELVES

UP DW

OPEN ABOVE

LIVING
RM
13⁴ x 11⁴

FOYER

PDR

COVERED PORCH

First Floor

BEDRM
15⁴ x 11⁸

BEDRM
11⁶ x 11⁰

BATH

LINEN

DN

Second Floor

QUOTE ONE®
Cost to build? See page 182
to order complete cost estimate
to build this house in your area!

DESIGN HPT150041

Square Footage: 1,484
Bonus Room: 484 sq. ft.
Width: 38'-0"
Depth: 70'-0"

Ideal for narrow lots, this fine bungalow home is full of amenities. The entry is just off a covered front porch and leads to a living room complete with a fireplace. The formal dining room is nearby, and works well with the L-shaped kitchen. The sleeping zone consists of a master suite with a walk-in closet and private bath, as well as two family bedrooms sharing a full bath. An unfinished attic waits for future developments while a two-car garage easily shelters the family fleet.

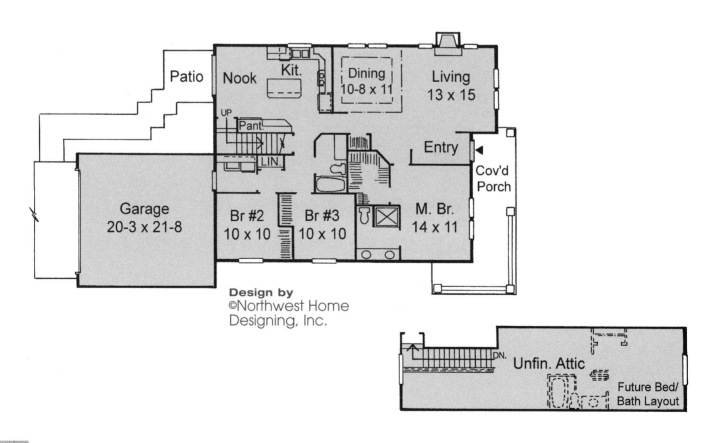

Patio
Nook
Kit.
Dining
10-8 x 11
Living
13 x 15
UP
Pant
Entry
Cov'd
Porch
Garage
20-3 x 21-8
Br #2
10 x 10
Br #3
10 x 10
M. Br.
14 x 11
LIN

Design by
©Northwest Home
Designing, Inc.

DN.
Unfin. Attic
Future Bed/
Bath Layout

P illars, gables, shingles and stone—all elements of the fine Craftsman style—create a stunning facade for this design. This comfortable 1½ story home will enhance any neighborhood. The entry is flanked by a formal dining room to the right and a spacious great room on the left. Here, a warming fireplace adds cheer to any gathering. The U-shaped kitchen features a snack bar, large pantry and adjacent nook with rear-yard access. Located on the first floor for privacy, the master bedroom is designed to pamper. Complete with a walk-in closet and a sumptuous bath, this suite guarantees relaxation.

DESIGN HPT150042

First Floor: 1,365 sq. ft.
Second Floor: 518 sq. ft.
Total: 1,883 sq. ft.
Width: 54'-4"
Depth: 46'-0"

Design by
©Ahmann Design, Inc.

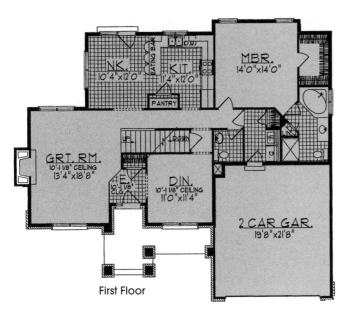

First Floor

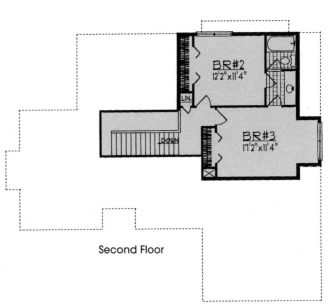

Second Floor

SHINGLE STYLE

DESIGN HPT150043

Square Footage: 1,997
Width: 60'-0"
Depth: 51'-0"

Design by
©Alan Mascord Design
Associates, Inc.

Elements of the Shingle style reside in this lovely traditional home, which captures a sense of casual dignity. The foyer opens to the formal rooms and to a secluded den or guest room. A vaulted family room adjoins a galley-style kitchen and a morning nook that accesses the outdoors. Sleeping quarters are connected by a hall leading back to the foyer. The master bedroom enjoys a private bath—with garden tub, separate shower, dual basins and a compartmented toilet—and a walk-in closet. The laundry room provides convenient access to the three-car garage.

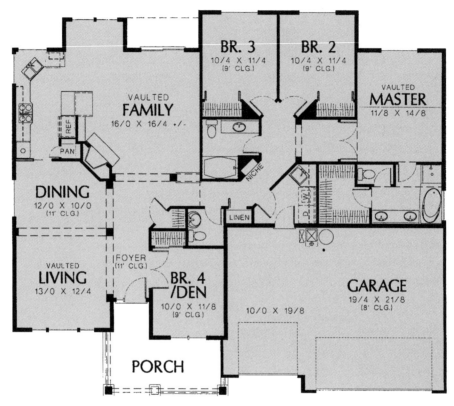

VAULTED
FAMILY
16/0 X 16/4 +/-

BR. 3
10/4 X 11/4
(9' CLG.)

BR. 2
10/4 X 11/4
(9' CLG.)

VAULTED
MASTER
11/8 X 14/8

REF
PAN

DINING
12/0 X 10/0
(11' CLG.)

NICHE

LINEN

FOYER
(11' CLG.)

VAULTED
LIVING
13/0 X 12/4

BR. 4
/DEN
10/0 X 11/8
(9' CLG.)

GARAGE
19/4 X 21/8
(8' CLG.)

10/0 X 19/8

PORCH

Shingles and siding are set off by two lovely gables and a charming covered porch on this stylish traditional home. Formal rooms and a quiet study with built-in bookshelves flank the foyer. The living room is enhanced with a vaulted ceiling and muntin windows that provide views to the front of the property. A morning nook opens to the family room and the kitchen. Two secondary bedrooms are connected to the master bedroom by a hall which also offers a full bath. The master bedroom boasts a vaulted ceiling, expansive walk-in closet, compartmented toilet and separate tub and shower.

DESIGN HPT150044

Square Footage: 1,999
Width: 60'-0"
Depth: 52'-0"

Design by
©Alan Mascord Design Associates, Inc.

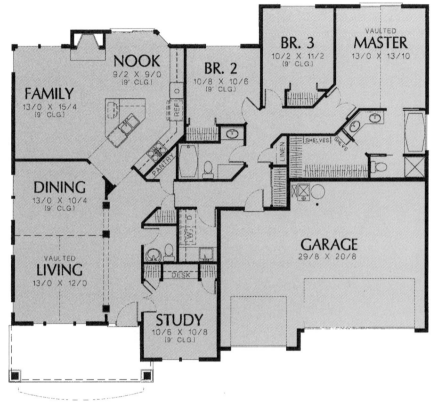

NOOK
9/2 X 9/0
(9' CLG.)

FAMILY
13/0 X 15/4
(9' CLG.)

BR. 2
10/8 X 10/6
(9' CLG.)

BR. 3
10/2 X 11/2
(9' CLG.)

MASTER
VAULTED
13/0 X 13/10

REFR.

PANTRY

DINING
13/0 X 10/4
(9' CLG.)

SHELVES   SHLVS

LINEN

VAULTED
LIVING
13/0 X 12/0

W/D

DESK

GARAGE
29/8 X 20/8

STUDY
10/6 X 10/8
(9' CLG.)

DESIGN HPT150045

First Floor: 1,198 sq. ft.
Second Floor: 668 sq. ft.
Total: 1,866 sq. ft.
Width: 40'-0"
Depth: 47'-0"

Design by
©Alan Mascord Design
Associates, Inc.

A fine example of a Craftsman bungalow, this four-bedroom home will be a delight to own. The efficient kitchen offers a serving island to the dining area, while the glow from the corner fireplace in the great room adds cheer to the entire area. Located on the first floor for privacy, the vaulted master bedroom features a walk-in closet, a private bath with a dual-bowl vanity, and access to the rear yard. Upstairs, three secondary bedrooms share a full hall bath and a large linen closet. The two-car garage will easily shelter the family fleet.

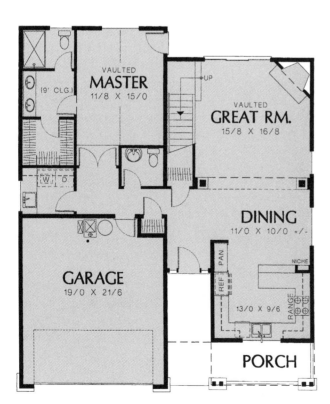

First Floor

Second Floor

This cute little bungalow will not only fit on a narrow lot, it also features many amenities. With shingles, rafter tails and pillars supporting a covered front porch, Craftsman influence is highly evident. Inside, the foyer opens directly to the living room, where a fireplace adds cheer to any gathering. The formal dining room offers fine ceiling detailing and easy access to the efficient kitchen. Two family bedrooms share a hall bath, while the master bedroom suite is complete with a walk-in closet and a private bath. The attic offers plenty of room for future expansion when it's needed.

DESIGN HPT150046

Square Footage: 1,506
Bonus Room: 621 sq. ft.
Width: 44'-0"
Depth: 53'-0"

Design by
©Northwest Home
Designing, Inc.

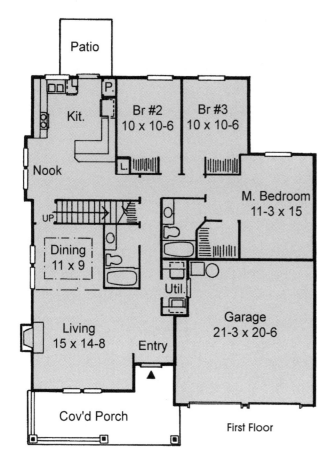

First Floor

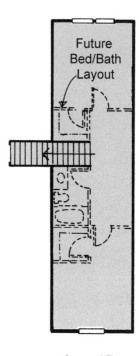

Second Floor

SHINGLE STYLE

DESIGN HPT150047

Square Footage: 1,888
Bonus Room: 358 sq. ft.
Width: 59'-8"
Depth: 57'-7"

Design by
Donald A. Gardner
Architects, Inc.

Here's a charming Bungalow cottage with room to grow. Split sleeping quarters place the master wing to the left of the plan, and the secondary bedrooms to the right. A side staircase leads to a sizable bonus room with two skylights. On the first floor, warmth from the central fireplace circulates through the open interior, set off by lovely views. The kitchen furnishes an island counter and serves a breakfast bay as well as an elegant formal dining room. The two-car garage offers additional storage space.

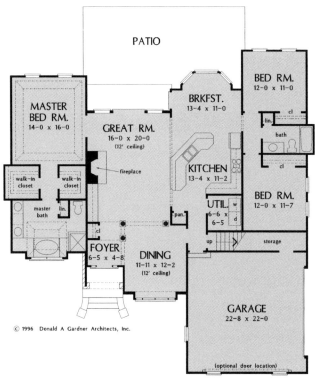

PATIO

MASTER BED RM.
14-0 x 16-0

GREAT RM.
16-0 x 20-0
(12' ceiling)

BRKFST.
13-4 x 11-0

BED RM.
12-0 x 11-0

fireplace

KITCHEN
13-4 x 11-2

bath

walk-in closet

walk-in closet

master bath

lin.

cl

BED RM.
12-0 x 11-7

UTIL.
6-6 x 6-5

pan.

FOYER
6-5 x 4-8

DINING
11-11 x 12-2
(12' ceiling)

up

storage

GARAGE
22-8 x 22-0

(optional door location)

© 1996 Donald A Gardner Architects, Inc.

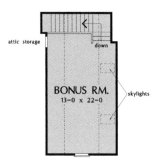

attic storage

down

BONUS RM.
13-0 x 22-0

skylights

A variety of exterior materials and interesting windows combine with an unusual floor plan to make this an exceptional home. Designed for a sloping lot, full living quarters dwell on the main level, but with two extra bedrooms and a family room added to the lower level. A covered porch showcases a wonderful dining-room window and an attractive front door. The living room, enhanced by a fireplace, adjoins the dining room for easy entertaining. The island kitchen and a bayed breakfast room are to the left. Three bedrooms on this level include one that is placed to serve as a study, and a master bedroom.

DESIGN HPT150048

Main Level: 2,297 sq. ft.
Lower Level: 1,212 sq. ft.
Total: 3,509 sq. ft.
Width: 70'-10"
Depth: 69'-0"

Design by
Donald A. Gardner
Architects, Inc.

Main Level

Lower Level

DESIGN HPT150049

Square Footage: 1,966
Bonus Room: 355 sq. ft.
Width: 62'-6"
Depth: 56'-10"

Design by
Donald A. Gardner
Architects, Inc.

Shingles, gables, stickwork and pillars all combine to give this home plenty of curb appeal. Inside, the foyer is flanked by a formal dining room and a study that could serve as a den. Defined by pillars, the dining room easily accesses the kitchen. A bayed breakfast room provides a pleasant place to have an early morning coffee break. The spacious great room features a fireplace and built-in shelves. The primary master bedroom includes a garden tub, separate shower, dual basins, a walk-in closet and a tray ceiling. An optional second master suite is located on the right side of the home.

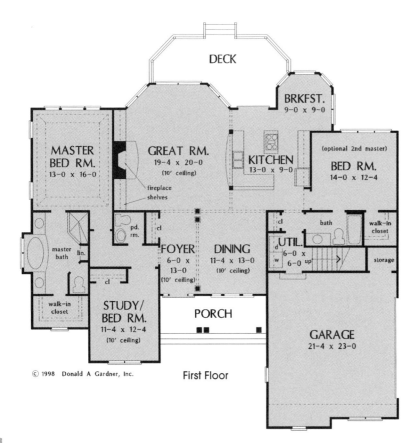

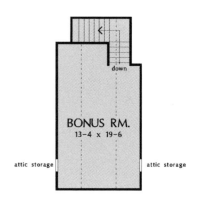

BONUS RM.
13-4 x 19-6

attic storage   attic storage

© 1998 Donald A Gardner, Inc.   First Floor

C edar shakes, siding and stone blend with the Craftsman details of a custom design in this stunning home. The plan's open design and non-linear layout is refreshing and functional. The second-floor loft overlooks a centrally located and vaulted great room, and the breakfast area with tray ceiling is virtually surrounded by windows to enhance the morning's light. The first-floor master suite is secluded and features a bay window, tray ceiling, walk-in closet and private bath. The second-floor family bedrooms are illuminated by rear dormers. A first-floor bedroom/study and a bonus room with second-floor access add flexibility.

DESIGN HPT150050

First Floor: 1,580 sq. ft.
Second Floor: 627 sq. ft.
Total: 2,207 sq. ft.
Width: 64'-2"
Depth: 53'-4"

Design by
Donald A. Gardner
Architects, Inc.

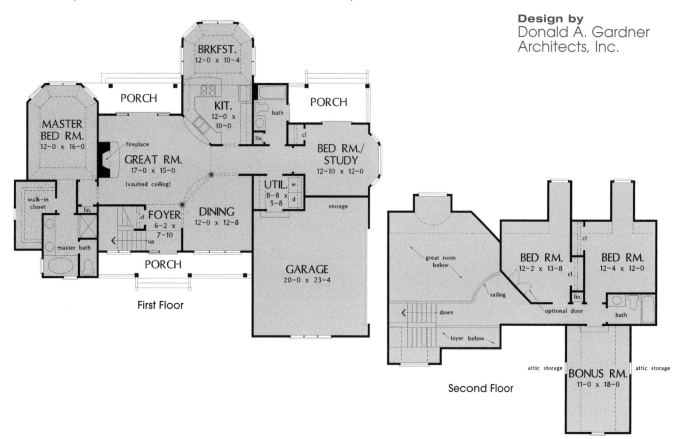

First Floor

Second Floor

SHINGLE STYLE

DESIGN HPT150051

Square Footage: 2,290
Bonus Room: 355 sq. ft.
Width: 53'-0"
Depth: 77'-10"

An appealing mixture of exterior building materials combines with decorative wood brackets in the gables to create undeniable Craftsman style for this four-bedroom home. Special ceiling treatments create volume and add interest throughout the home: tray ceilings in the foyer, dining room, bedroom/study and a master bedroom and a stunning cathedral ceiling in the great room. The great room is further enhanced by a rear clerestory dormer window and back-porch access. Bay windows expand several key rooms: the dining room, breakfast area, bedroom/study and the master bedroom's sitting area. His and Hers walk-in closets, back-porch access and a lavish bath augment the master suite. Three more bedrooms, two full baths and a bonus room complete the home.

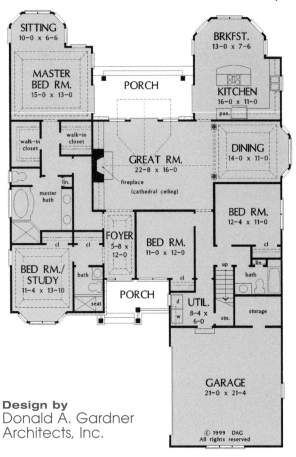

SITTING
10-0 x 6-6

MASTER
BED RM.
15-0 x 13-0

PORCH

walk-in closet

walk-in closet

master bath

GREAT RM.
22-8 x 16-0

fireplace
(cathedral ceiling)

BRKFST.
13-0 x 7-6

KITCHEN
16-0 x 11-0

pan.

DINING
14-0 x 11-0

BED RM.
12-4 x 11-0

lin.

cl

FOYER
5-8 x 12-0

BED RM.
11-0 x 12-0

lin.

bath

BED RM./
STUDY
11-4 x 13-10

bath

seat

PORCH

up

UTIL.
8-4 x 6-0

d
w

sto.

storage

cl

GARAGE
21-0 x 21-4

Design by
Donald A. Gardner
Architects, Inc.

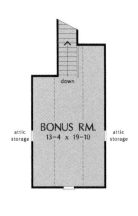

down

BONUS RM.
13-4 x 19-10

attic storage

attic storage

Gables, horizontal and vertical siding and cedar shakes combine with an inviting and arched L-shaped porch to captivate this Craftsman-style home. The cathedral ceiling heightens the great room, while the dining room receives refinement from an elegant tray ceiling. A bay window invites sunlight into the breakfast room and kitchen. Two family bedrooms share a spacious bath—with double sinks—on one side of the home, giving the master bedroom ultimate privacy on the other. The master bedroom features back-porch access, ample closet space and a roomy private bath, plus access to the rear step-down porch. Note the bedroom/study's front-porch entryway.

DESIGN HPT150052

Square Footage: 2,124
Bonus Room: 296 sq. ft.
Width: 57'-4"
Depth: 68'-8"

Design by
Donald A. Gardner
Architects, Inc.

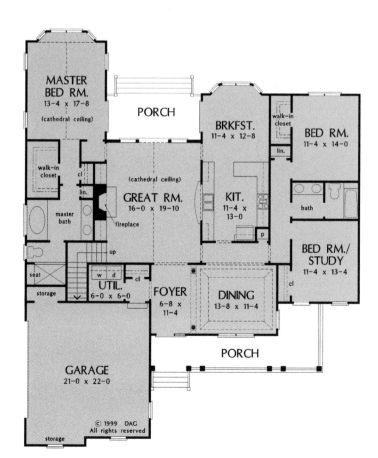

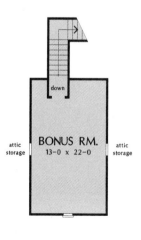

DESIGN HPT150053

Square Footage: 1,643
Bonus Room: 290 sq. ft.
Width: 51'-0"
Depth: 57'-0"

Design by
©Northwest Home
Designing, Inc.

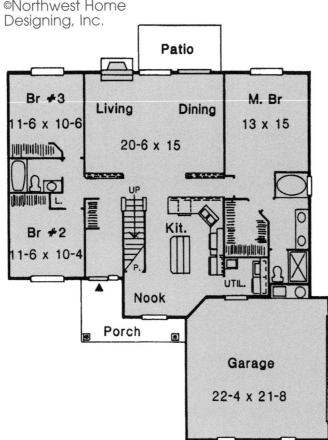

This fine Craftsman bungalow will look good in any neighborhood and will surely be a family favorite. Entertaining will be a breeze with the open living and dining area, which is highlighted by a fireplace and access to the rear patio. The L-shaped kitchen offers a large island and an adjacent nook for casual times. Split bedrooms ensure privacy, with the sumptuous master suite on the right side of the home and two family bedrooms on the left, sharing a full bath. The master suite is designed with amenities, including a walk-in closet and a separate tub and shower. The unfinished bonus space is available for future use as a home office, a playroom for kids, a media room or a guest suite.

A trio of gables adorn this fine three-bedroom bungalow. Accented by shingles and siding, with a welcoming porch, this fine home will dress up any neighborhood. Inside, the efficient kitchen easily serves the sunny nook as well as the family room. Patio access further enhances the appeal of the family room. A separate living room is available for formal gatherings. Upstairs, two family bedrooms share a full hall bath, while the master bedroom suite features a walk-in closet and a private bath. Note the large bonus room on this level—perfect for a playroom, study or fourth bedroom. The two-car garage has an option for a third-car bay.

DESIGN HPT150054

First Floor: 807 sq. ft.
Second Floor: 709 sq. ft.
Total: 1,516 sq. ft.
Bonus Room: 278 sq. ft.
Width: 42'-0"
Depth: 44'-0"

Design by
©Northwest Home
Designing, Inc.

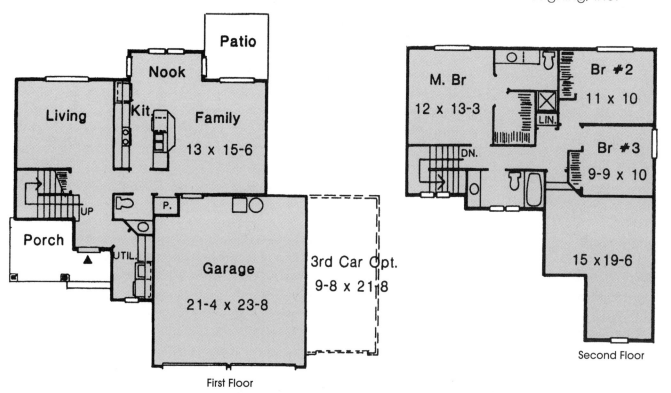

First Floor

Second Floor

DESIGN HPT150055

First Floor: 1,234 sq. ft.
Second Floor: 1,108 sq. ft.
Total: 2,342 sq. ft.
Width: 56'-0"
Depth: 74'-6"

This charming Craftsman home offers an intriguing and comfortable floor plan. A boxed window brightens the front parlor, which also includes a fireplace. Nine-foot ceilings throughout the first floor add an open, spacious feel to the plan. An island kitchen serves the dining room and the breakfast nook with ease. Double doors in the breakfast nook open to the rear yard. Upstairs, a vaulted ceiling in the master bedroom gives a feeling of luxury, as does the adjoining bath. Two additional bedrooms share a full bath and a linen closet; a fourth bedroom can double as a den.

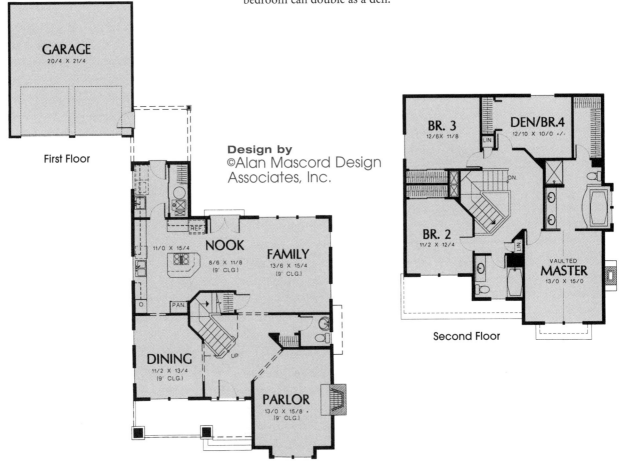

GARAGE
20/4 X 21/4

First Floor

Design by
©Alan Mascord Design
Associates, Inc.

NOOK
8/6 X 11/8

FAMILY
13/6 X 15/4
(9' CLG.)

REF.
11/0 X 15/4

PAN.

UP

DINING
11/2 X 13/4
(9' CLG.)

PARLOR
13/0 X 15/8
(9' CLG.)

BR. 3
12/6X 11/8

DEN/BR.4
12/10 X 10/0 +/-

LIN

DN.

BR. 2
11/2 X 12/4

LIN

VAULTED
MASTER
13/0 X 15/0

Second Floor

The combination of shingle and stone adds character to the facade of this charming two-story Craftsman home. Inside is a design that possesses great economy of space. The dining and living rooms, directly off the foyer, are beautifully accented by pillars. The family room allows for more intimate entertaining at the rear of the first floor. A den is found off the family room and opens to its own private patio. The second floor boasts three family bedrooms, sharing a full bath, in addition to a lavish master bedroom. The master bath includes a double-sink vanity, compartmented toilet, bath, shower and walk-in closet.

DESIGN HPT150056

First Floor: 1,562 sq. ft.
Second Floor: 1,384 sq. ft.
Total: 2,946 sq. ft.
Width: 52'-0"
Depth: 41'-0"

Design by
©Alan Mascord Design
Associates, Inc.

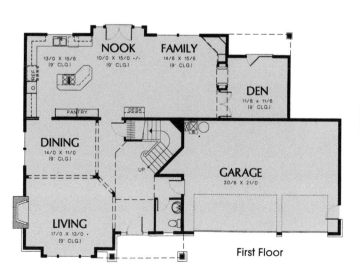

First Floor

Second Floor

SHINGLE STYLE

DESIGN HPT150057

First Floor: 1,200 sq. ft.
Second Floor: 1,339 sq. ft.
Total: 2,539 sq. ft.
Width: 56'-0"
Depth: 40'-0"

L

Design by
©Alan Mascord Design
Associates, Inc.

A covered front porch introduces this home's comfortable living pattern. The two-story foyer opens to a living room with a fireplace and lots of natural light. In the kitchen, an island cooktop, pantry, built-in planning desk and a nook with double doors to outside livability all aim to please. A spacious family room with another fireplace will accommodate casual living. Upstairs, five bedrooms—or four and a den—make room for all family members and guests. The master bedroom suite exudes elegance with a beautiful ceiling and a pampering spa bath. A full hall bath with a skylight and dual lavatories serves the secondary bedrooms.

Second Floor

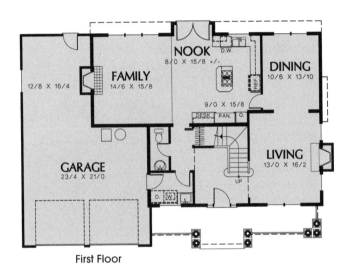

First Floor

Photo by Bob Greenspan

This home, as shown in the photograph, may differ from the actual blueprints. For more detailed information, please check the floor plans carefully.

Shingles, window detail, gabled rooflines and an attractively covered front porch all combine to give this home plenty of curb appeal. The floor plan inside is also an eye-catcher, with a U-shaped kitchen featuring a cooktop island and sharing a through-fireplace with the spacious great room. Here, a cathedral ceiling, a balcony from the second floor and access to the rear porch all enhance an already welcoming ambiance. Formal and casual meals are easily taken care of in either the dining room, with a box-bay window, or the unique breakfast room. Located on the first floor for privacy, the master suite is full of amenities. Two large second-floor bedrooms—both with window seats—share a full bath complete with a dual-bowl vanity.

DESIGN HPT150058

First Floor: 1,608 sq. ft.
Second Floor: 657 sq. ft.
Total: 2,265 sq. ft.
Width: 56'-4"
Depth: 70'-5"

Design by
Donald A. Gardner Architects, Inc.

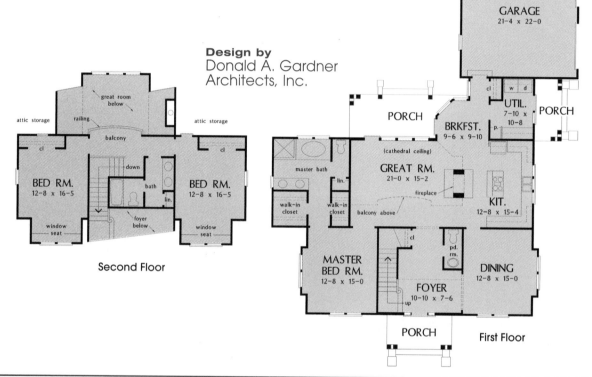

Second Floor

First Floor

DESIGN HPT150059

First Floor: 2,943 sq. ft.
Second Floor: 597 sq. ft.
Total: 3,540 sq. ft.
Width: 68'-0"
Depth: 97'-0"

Stone-and-shingle siding, gables, and columns framing the front entry all combine to give this home plenty of curb appeal. A two-story ceiling that starts in the foyer and runs through the great room gives a feeling of spaciousness. The great room is further enhanced by a built-in media center, a fireplace and direct access to the kitchen. Double doors lead into a vaulted den which also offers built-ins. Located on the first floor for privacy, the master bedroom is designed to pamper the homeowner. Here, amenities such as a huge walk-in closet, separate tub and shower and sliding glass doors to a rear porch make sure the homeowner is comfortable. Upstairs, two secondary bedrooms share a full hall bath.

Design by
©Alan Mascord Design Associates, Inc.

First Floor

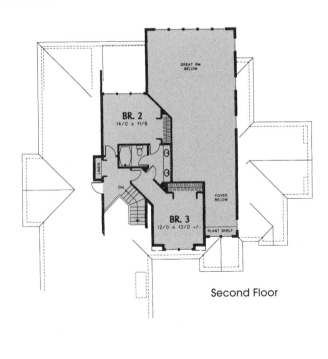

Second Floor

The rustic chic of Craftsman details makes this an unusual example of estate architecture. But, extravagant floor planning leaves no doubt that luxury is what this home is about. The first floor has open spaces for living: a reading room and dining room flanking the foyer, a huge family room with built-ins and a fireplace plus covered deck access, and an island kitchen and nook with a built-in table. The first-floor master suite is graced with a beamed ceiling. Its attached bath is well appointed and spacious. On the second floor are four bedrooms and three baths. Third-floor attic space can be used for whatever suits you best. Don't miss the home theater that can be developed in the basement and the home-office space over the garage.

DESIGN HPT150060

First Floor: 2,120 sq. ft.
Second Floor: 1,520 sq. ft.
Total: 3,640 sq. ft.
Basement: 377 sq. ft.
Width: 76'-0"
Depth: 81'-0"

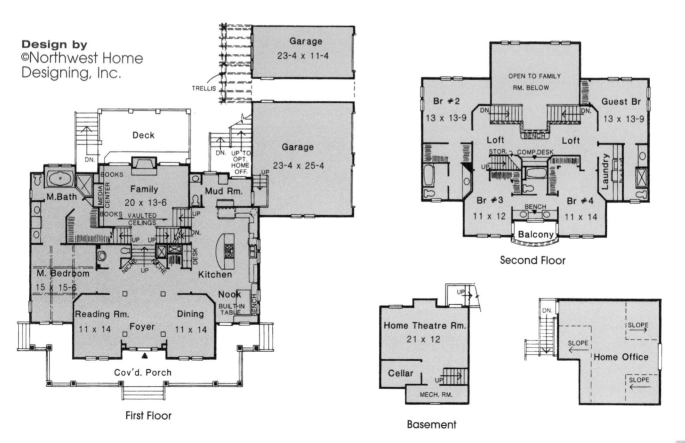

Design by
©Northwest Home Designing, Inc.

First Floor

Second Floor

Basement

SHINGLE STYLE

DESIGN HPT150061

First Floor: 1,640 sq. ft.
Second Floor: 711 sq. ft.
Total: 2,351 sq. ft.
Width: 51'-4"
Depth: 54'-0"

Design by
©Design Basics, Inc.

This home's cozy mix of cobblestone and shake siding brings to life the romance of an era long past. A wide, covered stoop leads to the entry showcased with twin coat closets and a see-through fireplace. A valley cathedral ceiling and stunning windows highlight the great room. The large kitchen features an island counter with a snack bar and quick access to the second floor via a rear stairway. The first-floor master bedroom takes up the left side of the plan—situated for privacy—and boasts a walk-in closet, a full bath and many other lavish amenities. Two bedrooms and a loft are upstairs.

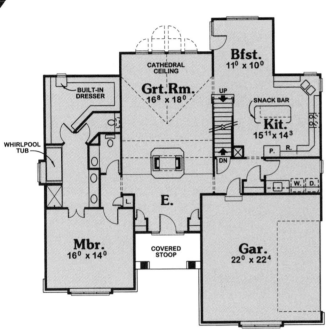

First Floor

Second Floor

Strong square pillars, a combination of shingles and siding and stylish window detailing dress up this fine Craftsman home. Inside, graceful detail continues, with an angled staircase echoed by the layout of the parlor and formal dining room. This home is designed to accommodate everyone. For quiet studying or working at home, there's the den at the front of the plan. The spacious family room is convenient to the L-shaped kitchen and offers a warming fireplace. Upstairs, three secondary bedrooms share a full hall bath, while the master suite is lavish with its luxuries. Completing this suite are two walk-in closets, a large and pampering bath and plenty of sunshine from the corner windows.

DESIGN HPT150062

First Floor: 1,158 sq. ft.
Second Floor: 1,044 sq. ft.
Total: 2,202 sq. ft.
Width: 54'-0"
Depth: 51'-0"

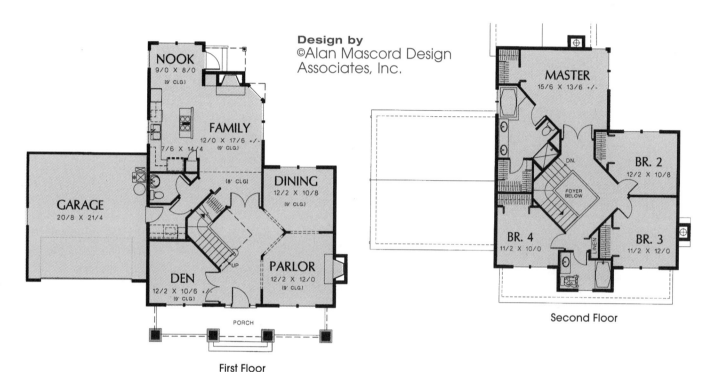

Design by
©Alan Mascord Design Associates, Inc.

First Floor

Second Floor

DESIGN HPT150063

First Floor: 1,054 sq. ft.
Second Floor: 1,306 sq. ft.
Total: 2,360 sq. ft.
Bonus Room: 220 sq. ft.
Width: 63'-0"
Depth: 42'-0"

Design by
©Northwest Home
Designing, Inc.

Shingles, siding, stone and fine detail give this home plenty of curb appeal. A covered front porch ushers you into the two-story foyer where an open staircase casually divides the home. To the left, a sunken living room waits, encouraging relaxation. To the right of the staircase, a hall leads back to the spacious family room which features a fireplace, access to the rear patio and an open layout with the kitchen. The second floor contains the sleeping zone. Three family bedrooms share a full bath, and a large bonus room is available for future expansion or as a playroom. A comfortable master suite includes a walk-in closet, private bath and balcony. The three-car garage is sure to shelter the family fleet.

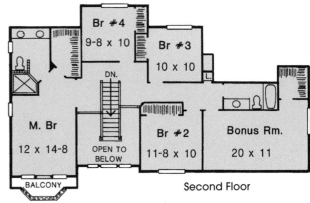

Second Floor

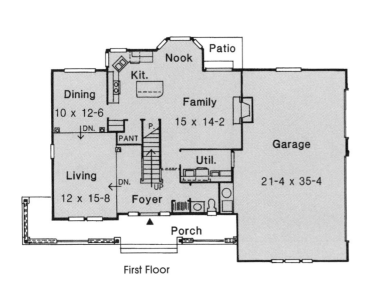

First Floor

COTTAGE INDUSTRY

*American and European-Style
cottage homes*

DESIGN HPT150064

Square Footage: 1,036
Optional Addition: 392 sq. ft.
Width: 37'-0"
Depth: 45'-0"

This quaint Victorian cottage offers beautiful detailing and the possibility of later additions. Enter into the living room that is open to the dining area and U-shaped kitchen. A utility room is located just off the kitchen. On the right, a family or guest bedroom is steps away from a full bath. The master suite features a full bath and walk-in closet. The future expansion offers two more secondary bedrooms and provides the master bedroom with two closets instead of a walk-in for a total addition of 392 square feet. The garage is optional.

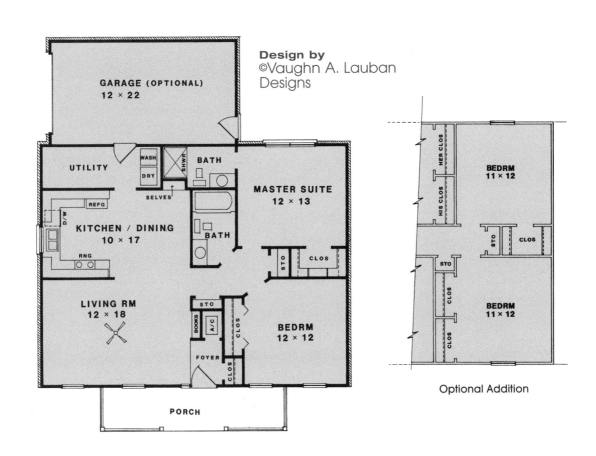

Design by
©Vaughn A. Lauban
Designs

A vaulted family room with a warming fireplace serves as the heart of this charming three-bedroom Folk Victorian design, where covered front and rear porches provide lots of out-door space. The formal dining room to the right of the foyer includes a coat closet and a storage area. A well-planned kitchen offers entrance to a utility room with another storage area. To the rear of the plan, the master bedroom provides a walk-in closet and a full bath with a dressing area. Two additional bedrooms, one with built-in shelves and a walk-in closet, share a full bath.

DESIGN HPT150065

Square Footage: 1,463
Width: 54'-0"
Depth: 60'-0"

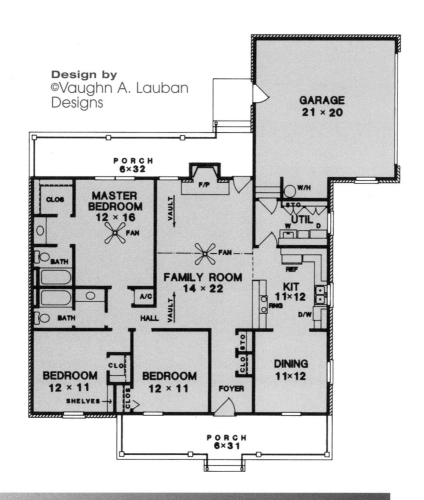

Design by
©Vaughn A. Lauban
Designs

GARAGE
21 × 20

PORCH
6×32

F/P

W/H
STO

UTIL
W   D

MASTER
BEDROOM
12 × 16
FAN

VAULT

REF

BATH

FAN

KIT
11×12

FAMILY ROOM
14 × 22

A/C

VAULT

RING

DINING
11×12

BATH

HALL

D/W

BEDROOM
12 × 11

CLO

BEDROOM
12 × 11

CLO
STO

SHELVES →

CLO

FOYER

PORCH
6×31

SHINGLE STYLE

DESIGN HPT150066

First Floor: 1,292 sq. ft.
Second Floor: 423 sq. ft.
Total: 1,715 sq. ft.
Width: 40'-0"
Depth: 59'-8"

Design by
Donald A. Gardner
Architects, Inc.

This narrow-lot plan is highlighted by an entrance with a barrel-vaulted ceiling and flanking detailed pillars. The great room and dining room share a vaulted ceiling to the second level. A spacious kitchen boasts an island and convenient breakfast area leading to the deck. The master bedroom on the main level has a large walk-in closet and a complete master bath including a double-bowl vanity, whirlpool tub, shower and linen storage. The second level accommodates two bedrooms, a full bath and a balcony as well as attic storage.

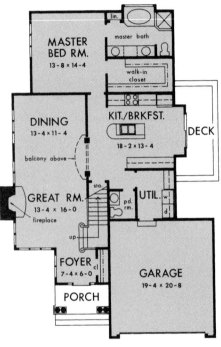

First Floor

Second Floor

Interesting arches, columns and cantilevers adorn this shingled home. A dining room with a tray ceiling flanks the foyer to the left, while a den/study flanks it to the right. A large living room enjoys rear views and the covered porch. The island kitchen has an abundance of counter space and directly flows into a bayed breakfast nook. The hearth-warmed family room boasts easy access to the kitchen. The master bedroom resides on the right side of the plan; amenities include His and Hers walk-in closets and sinks, a garden tub, separate shower, compartmented toilet and a sitting bay that looks to the rear porch. Bedrooms 2 and 3 on the left side of the plan share a walk-through full bath. A three-car garage and a bonus room, with bathroom facilities, complete this plan.

DESIGN HPT150067

Square Footage: 2,713
Bonus Room: 440 sq. ft.
Width: 66'-4"
Depth: 80'-8"

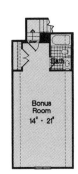

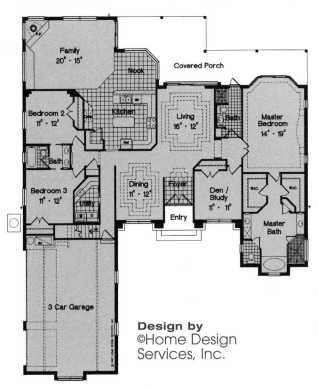

Family
20⁴ · 15⁸

Nook

Covered Porch

Kitchen

Living
16⁰ · 12⁰

Bath

Master Bedroom
14⁴ · 19⁰

Bedroom 2
11⁰ · 12⁰

Bath

Bonus Room
14⁰ · 21⁰

Bath

Bedroom 3
11⁰ · 12⁰

Utility

Dining
11⁰ · 12⁰

Foyer

Den / Study
11⁰ · 11⁰

W.I.C. W.I.C.

Entry

Master Bath

3 Car Garage

Design by
©Home Design
Services, Inc.

DESIGN HPT150068

First Floor: 2,070 sq. ft.
Second Floor: 790 sq. ft.
Total: 2,860 sq. ft.
Width: 57'-6"
Depth: 54'-0"

Wood shingles add a cozy touch to the exterior of this home; the arched covered front porch adds its own bit of warmth. Interior rooms include the great room with a bay window and a fireplace, the formal dining room and the study with another fireplace. A guest room on the first floor contains a full bath and walk-in closet. The relaxing master suite is also on the first floor and features a pampering master bath with His and Hers walk-in closets, dual vanities, a separate shower and a whirlpool tub just waiting to soothe and rejuvenate. The second floor holds two additional bedrooms, a loft area and a gallery which overlooks the central hall. This home is designed with a walkout basement foundation.

First Floor

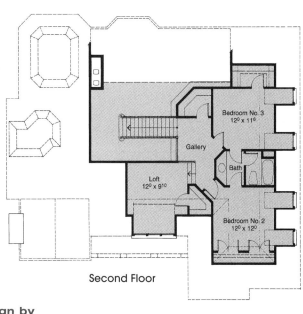

Second Floor

Design by
©Stephen Fuller, Inc.

The striking combination of wood frame, shingles and glass creates the exterior of this classic cottage. The foyer opens to the main-level layout. To the left of the foyer is a study with a warming hearth and vaulted ceiling, while to the right is a formal dining room. A great room with attached breakfast area sits to the rear near the kitchen. A guest room is nestled in the rear of the plan for privacy. The master suite provides an expansive tray ceiling, glass sitting area and easy passage to the outside deck. Upstairs, two bedrooms are accompanied by a loft for a quiet getaway. This home is designed with a walkout basement foundation.

DESIGN HPT150069

First Floor: 2,070 sq. ft.
Second Floor: 790 sq. ft.
Total: 2,860 sq. ft.
Width: 58'-4"
Depth: 54'-10"

QUOTE ONE®

Cost to build? See page 182
to order complete cost estimate
to build this house in your area!

First Floor

Design by
©Stephen Fuller, Inc.

Second Floor

DESIGN HPT150070

First Floor: 1,829 sq. ft.
Second Floor: 696 sq. ft.
Total: 2,525 sq. ft.
Width: 62'-0"
Depth: 53'-4"

This stunning four-bedroom home features a main-floor master suite for privacy and convenience. The master bath with a double vanity and whirlpool tub leads into a generous walk-in closet. The most notable feature of this home is the main living space with a see-through fireplace. On one side is a spacious great room with panoramic views to the rear. The other side boasts an open kitchen with a center island and abundant storage. The adjacent bumped-out nook has a volume ceiling admitting a shower of morning light. The three remaining bedrooms upstairs share a large full bath that includes a separate double vanity for busy mornings.

Design by
©Ahmann Design, Inc.

First Floor

Second Floor

Fieldstone and shingles give this exterior an upland country cottage look. The impressive entrance leads to a two-story foyer, filled with natural light. A gallery with a ten-foot ceiling leads further into the living room, which has rear-property views. The left side of the plan is devoted to a family room, with a fireplace, the island kitchen, utility room and breakfast area. The first-floor master suite boasts a vaulted ceiling, a private patio, His and Hers walk-in closets and dual basins. The second floor is home to three additional bedrooms, two full baths and a balcony that looks to the foyer below.

DESIGN HPT150071

First Floor: 2,036 sq. ft.
Second Floor: 866 sq. ft.
Total: 2,902 sq. ft.
Width: 65'-0"
Depth: 53'-4"

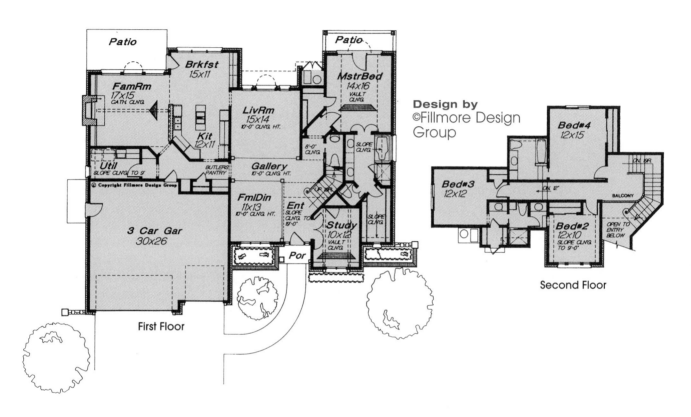

Design by
©Fillmore Design Group

First Floor

Second Floor

DESIGN HPT150072

Main Level: 2,213 sq. ft.
Lower Level: 1,333 sq. ft.
Total: 3,546 sq. ft.
Bonus Room: 430 sq. ft.
Width: 67'-2"
Depth: 93'-1"

Interesting window treatments highlight this stone-and-shake facade, but don't overlook the columned porch to the left of the portico. Arches outline the formal dining room and the family room, both of which are convenient to the island kitchen. Household chores are made easier by the placement of a pantry, powder room, laundry room and office between the kitchen and the entrances to the side porch and garage. If your goal is relaxation, the breakfast room, screened porch and covered deck are also nearby. The pampering master bedroom is to the left of the main level, with three more bedrooms and a recreation room on the lower level. A bonus room above the garage receives natural light from a dormer window.

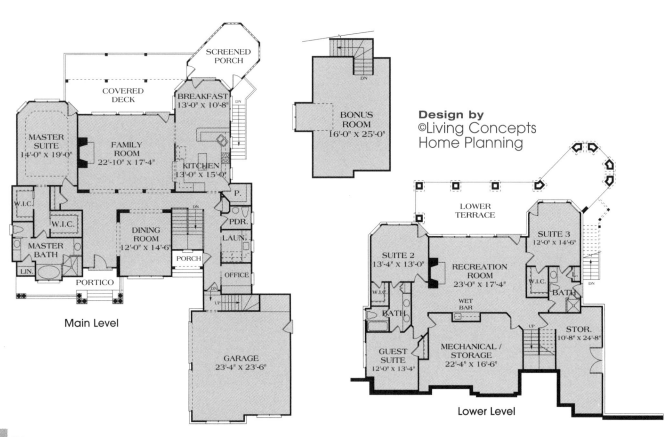

Design by
©Living Concepts
Home Planning

Design HPT150073

Square Footage: 2,770
Width: 73'-6"
Depth: 78'-0"

DECK

SITTING
12'-0"x 12'-0"

W.I.C.

**MASTER
BATH**

BREAKFAST
12'-0"x 13'-6"

DN.

GREAT ROOM
20'-6"x 18'-6"

MASTER SUITE
16'-6"x 15'-0"

W.I.C.

KITCHEN
14'-3"x 13'-6"

POWDER

BEDROOM NO.3
12'-0"x 12'-0"

LAUNDRY
9'-0" X 8'-6"

DINING ROOM
13'-6" X 14'-6"

FOYER

BATH

STORAGE

STOOP

BEDROOM NO.2
12'-3"x 14'-6"

TWO CAR GARAGE
21'-6"x 27'-6"

Design by
©Stephen Fuller, Inc.

This English cottage with a cedar shake exterior displays the best qualities of a traditional design. With the bay window and recessed entry, visitors will feel warmly welcomed. The foyer opens to both the dining room and the great room with its fireplace and built-in cabinetry. Surrounded by windows, the breakfast room opens to a gourmet kitchen and a laundry room conveniently located near the garage entrance. To the right of the foyer is a hall powder room. Two bedrooms with large closets are joined by a full bath with individual vanities and a window seat. Through double doors at the end of a short hall, the master suite awaits with a tray ceiling and an adjoining sunlit sitting room. The master bath features His and Hers closets, separate vanities, an individual shower and a garden tub with a bay window. This home is designed with a walkout basement foundation.

SHINGLE STYLE

QUOTE ONE®
Cost to build? See page 182
to order complete cost estimate
to build this house in your area!

PORCH

MASTER
BATH

MASTER BEDROOM
16'-4" X 13'-6"

BREAKFAST
13'-4" X 9'-0"

BEDROOM/
OFFICE
10'-4" X 11'-0"

GREAT ROOM
17'-0" X 17'-8"

BEDROOM NO. 2
10'-4" X 12'-0"

KITCHEN
13'-4" X 10'-6"

DN

BATH

LAUNDRY

BATH

DINING ROOM
11'-4" X 12'-10"

FOYER
5'-4" X
12'-10"

BEDROOM/
STUDY
11'-2" X 12'-0"

TWO CAR GARAGE
20'-6" X 19'-6"

PORCH

Design by
©Stephen Fuller, Inc.

DESIGN HPT150075

Square Footage: 2,090
Width: 61'-0"
Depth: 70'-6"

This traditional home features board-and-batten and cedar shingles in an attractively proportioned exterior. Finishing touches include a covered entrance, a porch with column detailing, arched transom, flower boxes and shuttered windows. The foyer opens to both the dining room and the great room beyond, with French doors accessing the porch. To the right of the foyer is the combination bedroom/study. A short hallway leads to a full bath and a secondary bedroom with ample closet space. The master bedroom is spacious, with walk-in closets on both sides of the entrance to the full bath. This home is designed with a walkout basement foundation.

DESIGN HPT150074

First Floor: 1,527 sq. ft.
Second Floor: 1,680 sq. ft.
Total: 3,207 sq. ft.
Width: 63'-6"
Depth: 62'-6"

Design by
©Stephen Fuller, Inc.

This engaging design blends the clean, sharp edges of the sophisticated shingle style with relaxed cottage details such as dove-coat gables and flower boxes. The rear of the plan takes advantage of rows of windows, allowing great views. The great room, with built-in bookshelves and a fireplace, opens to the kitchen and breakfast room, where a door leads to the deck. A spacious guest bedroom, also with access to the deck, has an adjoining bath and a walk-in closet. Upstairs, a study area provides a built-in desk. A dramatic master bedroom includes a bath with double vanities, a garden tub and a separate shower. Two bedrooms, one with a walk-in closet, share a full bath, while a third features a private bath. This home is designed with a walkout basement foundation.

First Floor

Second Floor

SHINGLE STYLE

DESIGN HPT150076

Square Footage: 2,366
Bonus Room: 622 sq. ft.
Width: 61'-10"
Depth: 62'-6"

Cedar shingles and brick give this home the flavor of a country cottage. Inside, an up-to-date floor plan includes all of today's amenities. Nine-foot ceilings throughout give the plan a spacious feel. The dining room is defined by elegant arched openings flanked by columns. A corner fireplace serves the great room with panache. The kitchen features lots of counter and cabinet space along with a walk-in pantry and a snack bar. Two secondary bedrooms share a hall bath. The optional second floor includes space for an additional bedroom, a bath and a large storage area over the garage. Please specify crawlspace or slab foundation when ordering.

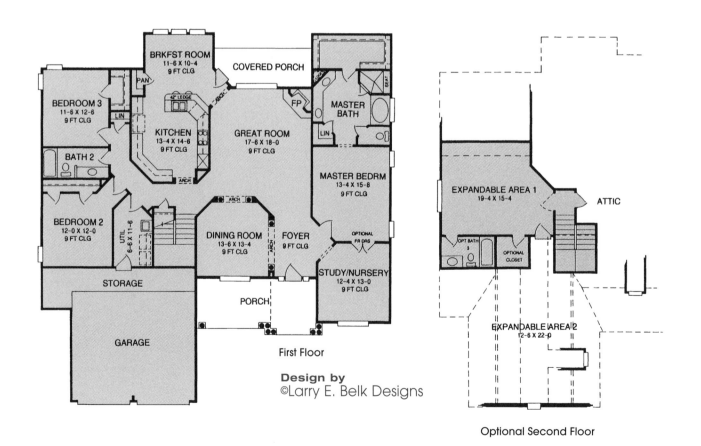

First Floor

Design by
©Larry E. Belk Designs

Optional Second Floor

Design HPT150077

Main Level: 2,153 sq. ft.
Lower Level: 1,564 sq. ft.
Basement Level: 794 sq. ft.
Total: 4,511 sq. ft.
Width: 68'-0"
Depth: 60'-0"

This elegant country cottage features shake siding with brick accents, charming gables and a gracious front porch. On the main level a spacious amenity-packed master suite dominates one whole side of the house and features oversized His and Hers closets, a walk-in shower and a long vanity with angled side mirrors. The foyer looks into the formal living room with a view to the rear deck that spans the full length of the house. The kitchen opens to the cozy breakfast/keeping room that doubles as a sun room due to all the windows. The lower level features one bedroom with a private bath and two others which share a Jack and Jill bath arrangement. The basement level offers the option of a fifth bedroom and bath, a recreation room and some basement storage.

Main Level

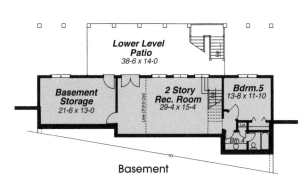

Basement

Lower Level

Design by
©Jannis Vann & Associates, Inc.

DESIGN HPT150078

Main Level: 2,546 sq. ft.
Lower Level: 1,814 sq. ft.
Total: 4,360 sq. ft.
Width: 66'-4"
Depth: 80'-8"

The facade of this home is a charming mixture of brick and shingles, with a cupola to complete the country feel. The vaulted great room—which looks to the rear terrace—is the center of this home, with the dining room flanking it to the right and the master bedroom to the left. The island kitchen accesses the screened porch and a laundry area. The first-floor master suite boasts a walk-in closet, garden tub, separate shower and a tray ceiling. An additional bedroom resides on this level as well. The lower level is resplendent with luxuries: a home theater, storage/workshop area, exercise room, recreation room, family suite, full bath, private bar and a covered terrace.

Design by
©Living Concepts
Home Planning

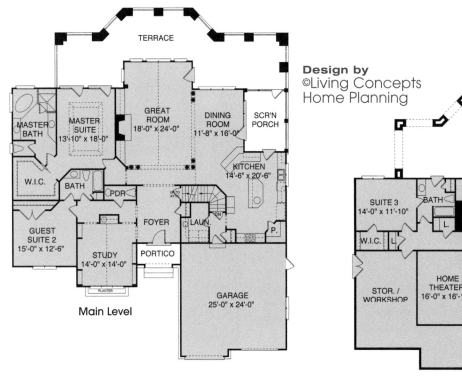

Main Level

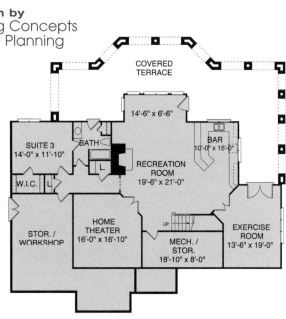

Lower Level

Muntin windows, keystone lintels and steeply pitched rooflines mark this home's exterior with grace and style. A dining room situated to the right of foyer is linked to the kitchen through a convenient door. The kitchen boasts a pantry and a nearby breakfast room, which looks to the rear property. The gathering room is enhanced with a fireplace and French doors to the backyard. The master suite, located on the first floor for privacy, includes many amenities a homeowner would love, including a garden tub, separate bath and compartmented toilet. Three suites reside upstairs, as do two full baths, an unfinished recreation room and a balcony that looks to the foyer below.

DESIGN HPT150079

First Floor: 1,867 sq. ft.
Second Floor: 1,090 sq. ft.
Total: 2,957 sq. ft.
Bonus Room: 424 sq. ft.
Width: 51'-4"
Depth: 68'-4"

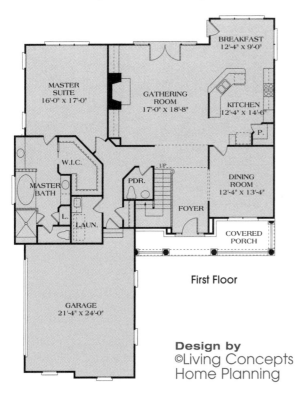

First Floor

Design by
©Living Concepts
Home Planning

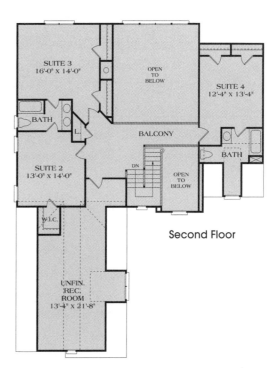

Second Floor

DESIGN HPT150080

First Floor: 774 sq. ft.
Second Floor: 723 sq. ft.
Total: 1,497 sq. ft.
Width: 42'-0"
Depth: 43'-0"

Shingles and siding combine to give this home a fine coastal feeling. The spacious gathering room has a fireplace and a French door to the back deck or patio. The L-shaped kitchen provides an ample pantry and plenty of counter space and easily accesses the formal dining room. A service entrance leads from the garage through the laundry room to the gathering room. The upper-level master suite has a walk-in closet, a double-bowl vanity and a garden tub. Two family bedrooms share a hall bath and complete this floor.

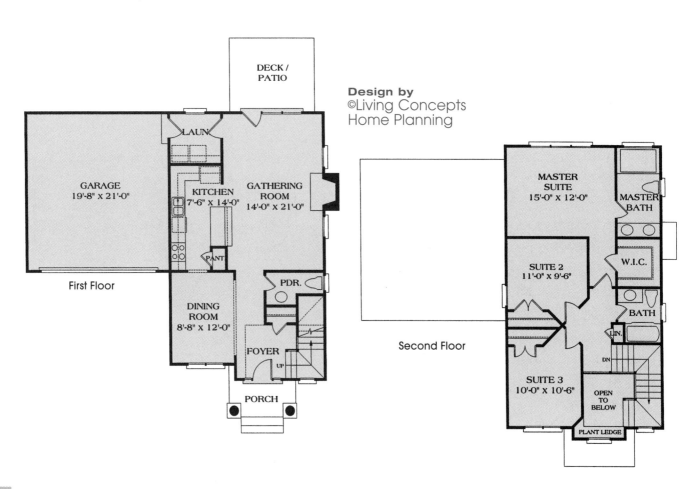

Design by
©Living Concepts
Home Planning

First Floor

DECK / PATIO

LAUN.

GARAGE
19'-8" x 21'-0"

KITCHEN
7'-6" x 14'-0"

GATHERING ROOM
14'-0" x 21'-0"

PANT.

PDR.

DINING ROOM
8'-8" x 12'-0"

FOYER

UP

PORCH

Second Floor

MASTER SUITE
15'-0" x 12'-0"

MASTER BATH

W.I.C.

SUITE 2
11'-0" x 9'-6"

BATH

LIN.

DN

SUITE 3
10'-0" x 10'-6"

OPEN TO BELOW

PLANT LEDGE

An open-plan layout gives this design maximum livability. A facade of siding and shingles creates an air of country charm, as does the second-floor flower box. Just past the entry foyer, a fireplace gives interest to the spacious gathering room, which flows into the dining area. Decorative columns separate it from the living area. A powder room, U-shaped kitchen and laundry complete the main level. Sleeping quarters on the second floor include two family bedrooms and a master suite with a walk-in closet and private bath. The two-car garage easily shelters the family fleet.

DESIGN HPT150081

First Floor: 817 sq. ft.
Second Floor: 759 sq. ft.
Total: 1,576 sq. ft.
Width: 43'-4"
Depth: 44'-6"

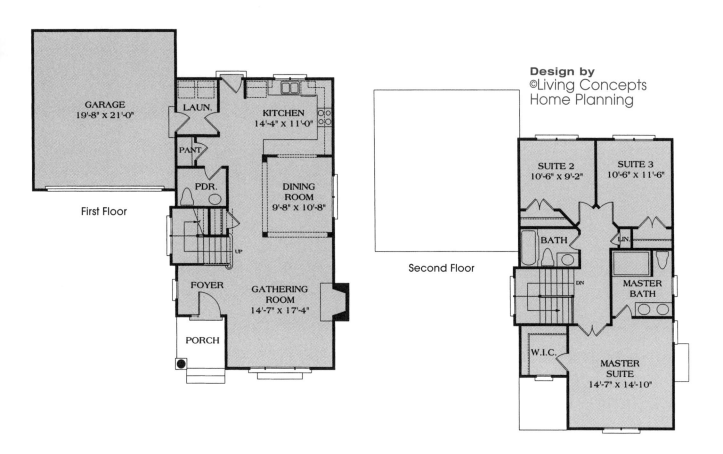

Design by
©Living Concepts
Home Planning

GARAGE
19'-8" x 21'-0"

LAUN.

KITCHEN
14'-4" x 11'-0"

PANT.

PDR.

DINING
ROOM
9'-8" x 10'-8"

First Floor

FOYER

GATHERING
ROOM
14'-7" x 17'-4"

UP

PORCH

Second Floor

SUITE 2
10'-6" x 9'-2"

SUITE 3
10'-6" x 11'-6"

BATH

LIN.

MASTER
BATH

DN

W.I.C.

MASTER
SUITE
14'-7" x 14'-10"

DESIGN HPT150082

First Floor: 2,228 sq. ft.
Second Floor: 1,099 sq. ft.
Total: 3,327 sq. ft.
Bonus Room: 648 sq. ft.
Width: 64'-4"
Depth: 79'-4"

This home presents elegance and English influence with its muntin windows, loggia, hipped rooflines and shingle detailing. Step inside, and the elegance continues with a foyer that leads directly to a cozy gathering room, complete with a fireplace and French-door access to the rear deck. The right side of the lower level is devoted to the island kitchen area, bayed breakfast nook, laundry room and sun room, which accesses a screened porch just off the deck. The left side of the plan houses the master suite, graced with His and Hers walk-in closets and a lovely full bath. Two additional family suites reside upstairs, along with the captain's quarters, a sun deck, another full bath and a rec room. The balcony overlooks the gathering room below, adding an air of spaciousness.

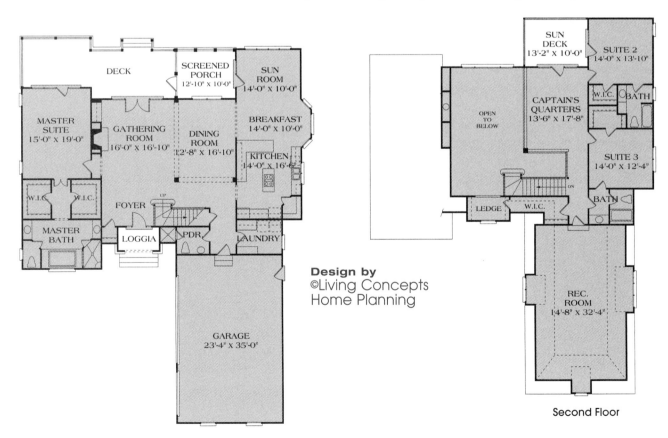

Design by
©Living Concepts
Home Planning

First Floor

Second Floor

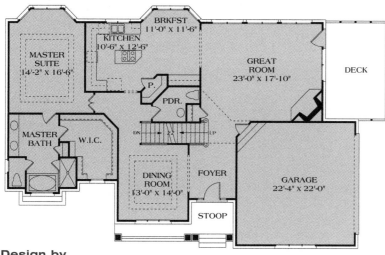

MASTER
SUITE
14'-2" X 16'-6"

BRKFST
11'-0" X 11'-6"

KITCHEN
10'-6" X 12'-6"

GREAT
ROOM
23'-0" X 17'-10"

DECK

P.

PDR.

MASTER
BATH

W.I.C.

DN UP

DINING
ROOM
13'-0" X 14'-0"

FOYER

GARAGE
22'-4" X 22'-0"

STOOP

Design by
©Living Concepts
Home Planning

First Floor

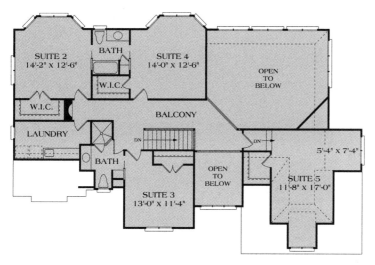

SUITE 2
14'-2" X 12'-6"

BATH

SUITE 4
14'-0" X 12'-6"

OPEN
TO
BELOW

W.I.C.

W.I.C.

BALCONY

LAUNDRY

DN

DN

5'-4" X 7'-4"

BATH

OPEN
TO
BELOW

SUITE 5
11'-8" X 17'-0"

SUITE 3
13'-0" X 11'-4"

Second Floor

Design HPT150083

First Floor: 1,790 sq. ft.
Second Floor: 1,484 sq. ft.
Total: 3,274 sq. ft.
Bonus Room: 391 sq. ft.
Width: 67'-0"
Depth: 44'-8"

Hipped rooflines, flower boxes and shed-style dormers serve to distinguish this home. Both the dining room and the master suite are graced with tray ceilings, lending a sense of increased spaciousness to the plan. The great room sits on the right side of the plan and offers a corner fireplace, an abundance of windows and access to a side deck. The U-shaped kitchen—complete with a cooktop island—nestles close to the bayed breakfast area and the first-floor powder room. Four family suites make up the second level. Suites 2 and 4 are graced with bay windows and a walk-through bath. Suites 3 and 5 share a hall bath. A laundry area is located conveniently near these bedrooms for easy washing.

DESIGN HPT150084

First Floor: 1,758 sq. ft.
Second Floor: 685 sq. ft.
Total: 2,443 sq. ft.
Bonus Room: 260 sq. ft.
Width: 55'-10"
Depth: 63'-6"

Craftsman-style windows and multiple gables enhance the appeal of this inviting coastal home. Inside, a spacious family room with a warming fireplace, flanked by built-ins, offers French-door access to the rear patio. Situated on the main level, the master suite is designed with a bayed sitting area and private access to the rear patio, as well as His and Hers walk-in closets, a garden tub, separate shower and twin-basin vanity. The upper level contains two suites—one with a private bath and one with unfinished storage—and a large bonus room.

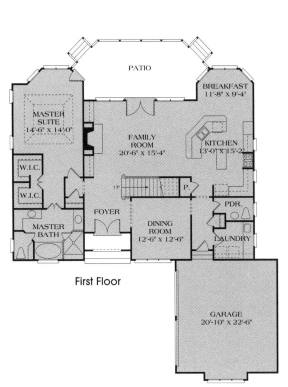

First Floor

Second Floor

Design by
©Living Concepts
Home Planning

A mixture of rooflines gives this shingle-style home a unique look. Enter through the covered porch, and to the right is the tray-ceilinged dining room. The great room—complete with a fireplace—is positioned at the rear of the house, away from street noise, and is granted backyard views through a set of windows. The kitchen is enhanced with a cooktop island, plenty of counter space and a nearby bayed breakfast nook and powder room. The first-floor master suite is situated at the back of the house for maximum privacy and boasts His and Hers walk-in closets, a bay window and many other amenities. The second level is home to three additional family suites—one with a balcony and the other two with bay windows—two full baths and a bonus room.

DESIGN HPT150085

First Floor: 1,890 sq. ft.
Second Floor: 1,286 sq. ft.
Total: 3,176 sq. ft.
Bonus Room: 431 sq. ft.
Width: 67'-0"
Depth: 56'-8"

Design by
©Living Concepts
Home Planning

First Floor

Second Floor

DESIGN HPT150086

First Floor: 2,620 sq. ft.
Second Floor: 2,001 sq. ft.
Total: 4,621 sq. ft.
Apartment: 673 sq. ft.
Width: 67'-0"
Depth: 103'-8"

With unique angles, brick detailing and double chimneys, this home is as sophisticated as it is comfortable. The foyer enters into a refined gallery, which runs past a dining room, complete with French doors opening to the front covered porch. The gallery also passes the grand room, which boasts a fireplace and three sets of French doors to the rear covered veranda. On the right, the master retreat provides its own private fireplace and access to the veranda. The kitchen and breakfast area is situated on the left side of the plan. Follow the steps up and an abundance of rooms will greet you. The recreation room directly accesses a small covered veranda. Two additional family suites flank the rec room, and each accesses a full bath. An apartment—perfect for renters or parents—and an office complete this floor.

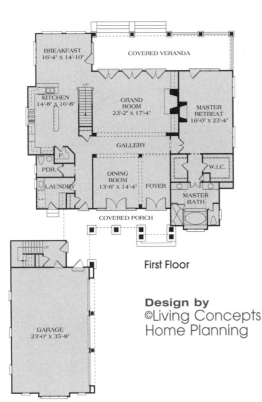

First Floor

Design by
©Living Concepts
Home Planning

Second Floor

This two-story home is replete with necessary components, as well as added luxuries. The master suite comprises the right side of the first level and includes His and Hers walk-in closets and a lavish full bath. The family room will be the center of attention in this home, with its tray ceiling, fireplace, rear-door access to the terrace and easy access to the kitchen. The kitchen is graced with plenty of counter space, a nearby bayed breakfast nook, laundry area, powder room and dining room. The second level is home to two family suites—one with a bay window—and two full baths. A recreation room and a bonus/learning center round out this plan.

DESIGN HPT150087

First Floor: 1,833 sq. ft.
Second Floor: 1,178 sq. ft.
Total: 3,011 sq. ft.
Bonus Room: 329 sq. ft.
Width: 75'-3"
Depth: 43'-2"

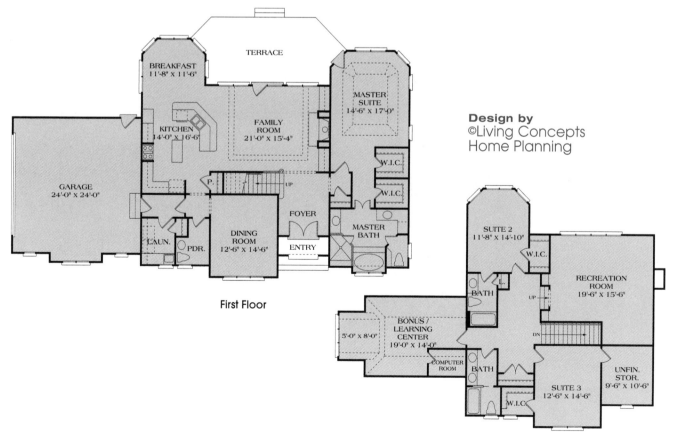

Design by
©Living Concepts
Home Planning

First Floor

Second Floor

SHINGLE STYLE

DESIGN HPT150088

First Floor: 2,430 sq. ft.
Second Floor: 1,624 sq. ft.
Total: 4,054 sq. ft.
Width: 70'-4"
Depth: 95'-9"

This charming home combines hipped rooflines, shingles and brickwork to create a design with European elements. Enter through the foyer, and to the left is a vaulted dining room with front property views. The gathering room—complete with a fireplace—and living room flank the kitchen. A bayed breakfast nook looks out to the lower rear terrace, and also enjoys close proximity to the kitchen. The first-floor master suite on the right side of the plan includes such amenities as a tray ceiling, His and Hers walk-in closets, a full bath, garden tub and separate shower. The second floor houses the remaining sleeping quarters. Suites 2 and 4 share a full bath, and each boasts balconies. Suite 3 enjoys a private bath and a walk-in closet. A partially vaulted playroom completes the second floor.

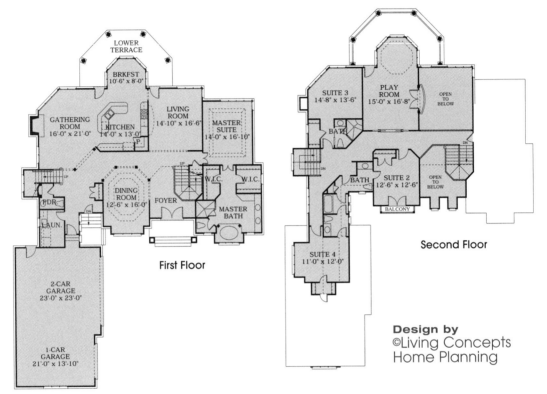

First Floor

Second Floor

Design by
©Living Concepts
Home Planning

Design HPT150089

Square Footage: 2,816
Guest House 290 sq. ft.
Bonus Room: 222 sq. ft.
Width: 113'-6"
Depth: 99'-6"

Floor Plan Labels

Pool
Bath 2
w.i.c.
Bedroom 2
Bath 3
Covered Patio
Family Room
Bedroom 3
w.i.c.
Master Suite
Parlor
Master Bath
Foyer
Bath
Lnd'ry
2 Car Garage
w.i.c.
w.i.c.
Pantry
Dining Room
Kitchen
Entry
Nook

Guest
Bath
w.i.c.
Garage

Sun Deck

Bonus Room

Design by
©Home Design
Services, Inc.

A striking front-facing pediment, bold columns and varying rooflines set this design apart from the rest. An angled entry leads to the foyer, flanked on one side by the dining room with a tray ceiling and on the other by a lavish master suite. This suite is enhanced with a private bath, two large walk-in closets, a garden tub, compartmented toilet and bidet, and access to the covered patio. The parlor also enjoys rear-yard views. From the breakfast nook and kitchen to the family room, the ceilings are vaulted, providing a sense of spaciousness. A laundry room and roomy pantry are accessible from the kitchen area. Two family bedrooms reside on the right side of the plan; each have their own full bath and are built at interesting angles. A vaulted bonus room includes French doors opening to a second-floor sun deck.

SHINGLE STYLE

DESIGN HPT150090

First Floor: 2,253 sq. ft.
Second Floor: 792 sq. ft.
Total: 3,045 sq. ft.
Width: 101'-4"
Depth: 59'-6"

This rambling, three-bedroom country design features a breezeway to the two-car garage, two fireplaces and the ultimate in master bedroom suites. The imposing living room, open to the second floor, features a fireplace flanked by built-in bookshelves and double doors to the curved rear terrace. A second fireplace in the family room backs to the terrace barbecue. The island kitchen opens to both the family room and the dining room. The master bedroom suite is centered between a study in the front and a private screened porch in the back, and includes a separate bath with His and Hers walk-in closets and vanities.

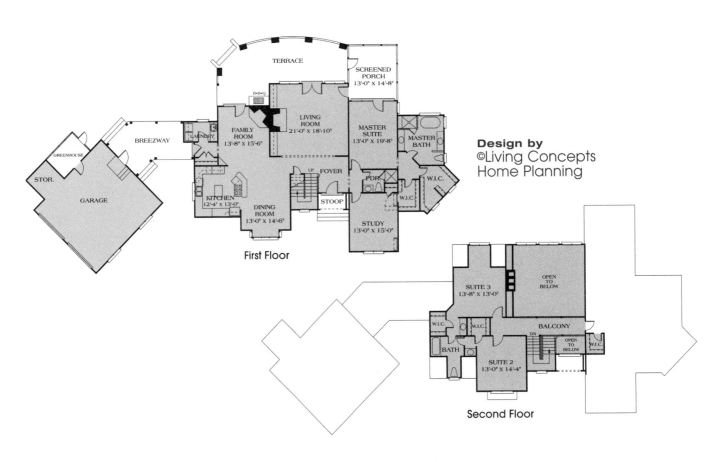

Design by
©Living Concepts
Home Planning

First Floor

Second Floor

With a wall of windows across the rear of the house, this design is ideal for a spot with breathtaking views. The stone-and-shake exterior gives a rustic look that is a welcome sight anywhere. An attractive recessed entry opens to a great room that dominates the living area. A fireplace and bookshelves make the great room a welcome spot when the temperature drops, while the deck and screened porch beckon during warmer weather. The kitchen opens into a large breakfast room for mealtimes, with a snack bar available for meals on the go. The first-floor master suite includes a walk-in closet and a compartmented bath with twin vanities. Two family bedrooms have private entrances to a shared bath at one end of the second-floor balcony, which overlooks the great room and leads to a loft area with another full bath.

DESIGN HPT150091

First Floor: 1,793 sq. ft.
Second Floor: 1,115 sq. ft.
Total: 2,918 sq. ft.
Width: 103'-8"
Depth: 57'-6"

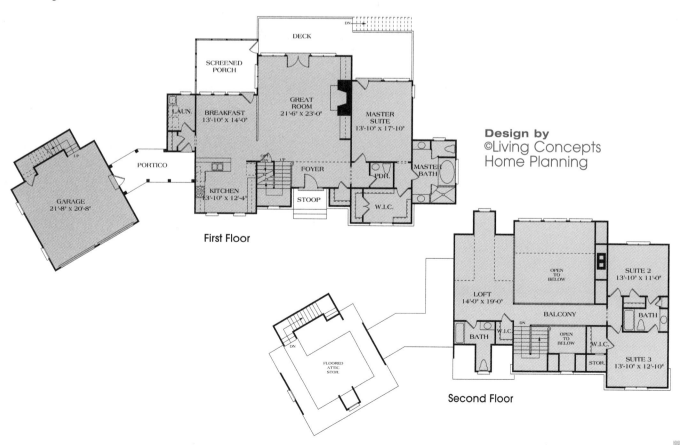

Design by
©Living Concepts
Home Planning

First Floor

Second Floor

SHINGLE STYLE

DESIGN HPT150092

First Floor: 2,122 sq. ft.
Second Floor: 719 sq. ft.
Total: 2,841 sq. ft.
Bonus Room: 535 sq. ft.
Width: 117'-0"
Depth: 57'-2"

A combination of stacked river stone and cedar shakes gives warmth and character to this English country facade. A vaulted ceiling adds height and spaciousness to the great room, which opens to the dining room for effortless entertaining. A fireplace and a built-in wet bar are welcome additions to the area, as is easy access to a covered deck. A side door near the kitchen opens to a breezeway leading to the garage. A study with a fireplace is a quiet spot, conveniently close to the master suite, which boasts a deluxe bath and a private door to the deck. A guest suite is located to the left of the foyer, where stairs lead up to the second floor and two more bedroom suites. There's plenty of storage on this level, as well as a loft that can serve many purposes.

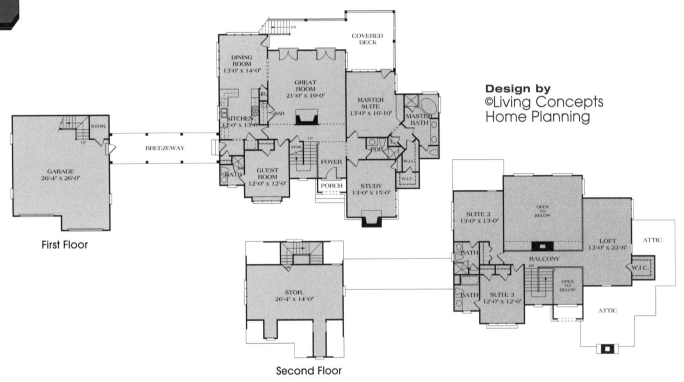

Design by
©Living Concepts
Home Planning

First Floor

Second Floor

S tepped gables, an exterior chimney and an open breezeway combine to give this English beauty outstanding curb appeal. The two-story grand room is the heart of the home for both formal entertaining and family relaxing. Amenities include a massive corner fireplace, a built-in wet bar and three doors to the back patio. The island kitchen, with a walk-in pantry and a snack bar, opens to the breakfast area, which accesses the skylit covered porch. A deluxe master suite, a nearby study with a fireplace and the formal dining room complete the first floor. Upstairs are two family bedrooms with private baths, and a balcony overlooking the grand room, and storage space. Unfinished areas over the garage and in the basement are available for future expansion.

DESIGN HPT150093

First Floor: 2,689 sq. ft.
Second Floor: 1,180 sq. ft.
Total: 3,869 sq. ft.
Bonus Room: 723 sq. ft.
Width: 126'-7"
Depth: 86'-0"

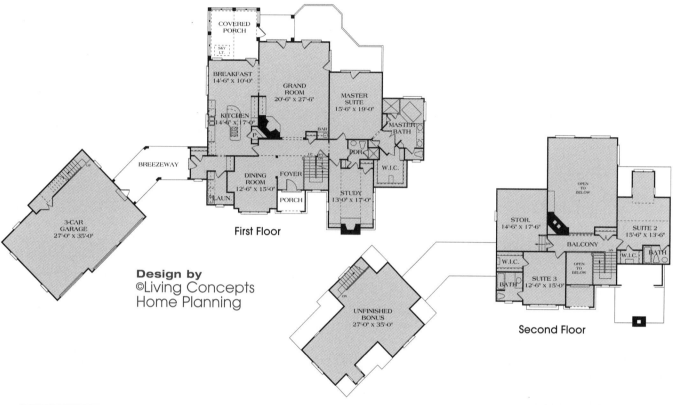

First Floor

Design by
©Living Concepts
Home Planning

Second Floor

DESIGN HPT150094

First Floor: 2,935 sq. ft.
Second Floor: 1,472 sq. ft.
Total: 4,407 sq. ft.
Width: 69'-4"
Depth: 76'-8"

A mixture of hipped and gabled rooflines lend this design an air of Old World sophistication. A beautiful Palladian window enhances the curb appeal of this home. A raised foyer leads into a living room graced with a volume ceiling and a wall of windows that looks to the covered patio. The large master bedroom boasts a volume ceiling, French doors to the covered patio, a private sitting area, a fireplace, two walk-in closets and a spacious private bath. A vaulted family room enjoys a central fireplace, built-ins and an abundance of windows. The large island kitchen leads to a breakfast area and a convenient utility room. A grand staircase leads to the sleeping quarters above, including three family bedrooms, a vaulted media room and a loft that looks to the family and living rooms below. Bedroom 4 is graced with a private deck and bath, while Bedrooms 2 and 3 share a walk-through bath.

Design by
©Home Design Services, Inc.

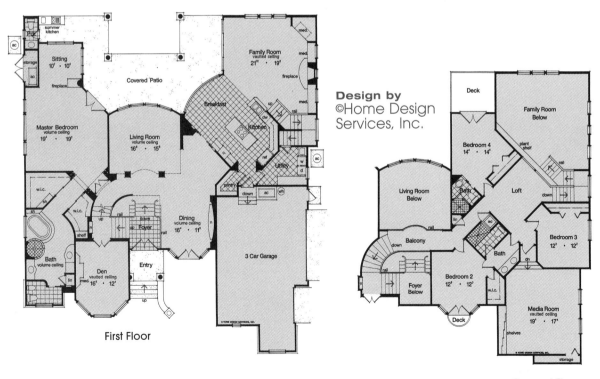

First Floor

Second Floor

COUNTRY STYLE

Victorian and Farmhouse designs

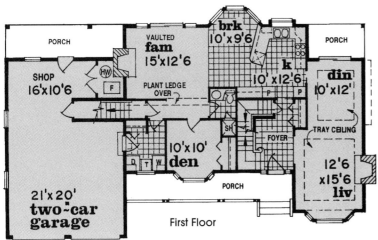

First Floor

PORCH

VAULTED
fam
15'x12'6

brk
10'x9'6

PORCH

SHOP
16'x10'6

HW

F

PLANT LEDGE
OVER

k
10' x12'6

din
10'x12'

SH

FOYER

TRAY CEILING

10'x10'
den

D   T   W

12'6
x15'6
liv

21'x20'
**two-car
garage**

PORCH

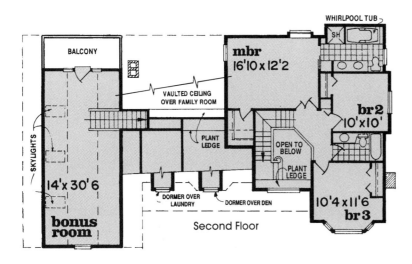

Second Floor

WHIRLPOOL TUB

BALCONY

SKYLIGHTS

VAULTED CEILING
OVER FAMILY ROOM

mbr
16'10 x 12'2

SH

14'x30'6

PLANT
LEDGE

OPEN TO
BELOW

PLANT
LEDGE

br2
10'x10'

**bonus
room**

DORMER OVER
LAUNDRY

DORMER OVER DEN

10'4 x11'6
br3

DESIGN HPT150095

First Floor: 1,233 sq. ft.
Second Floor: 797 sq. ft.
Total: 2,030 sq. ft.
Bonus Room: 427 sq. ft.
Width: 66'-6"
Depth: 40'-6"

A covered railed porch, dormer windows and fish-scale siding accent this charming country plan. The spacious interior offers both formal and informal areas: living and dining rooms with tray ceilings, vaulted family room and bayed breakfast room. Both the living room and family room are warmed by fireplaces. A cozy den sits just to the left of the foyer. Three bedrooms are found on the second floor, including the well-appointed master suite. A large skylit bonus room available for future development features a balcony overlooking the rear yard.

Design by
©Select Home Designs

With stylish details borrowed from Craftsman, Victorian and farmhouse styles, this design is elegant without being pretentious. The entry opens to a two-story foyer which holds a half-bath, coat closet and stairs to the second floor. The living and dining rooms are on the right and the dining room includes a buffet alcove. A family room is in the opposite corner and features patio access. Both the family room and the living room have fireplaces. The second-floor master bedroom boasts a walk-in closet, twin-basin vanity and separate tub and shower. Three family bedrooms and one full bath complete the second floor.

DESIGN HPT150096

First Floor: 1,100 sq. ft.
Second Floor: 1,016 sq. ft.
Total: 2,116 sq. ft.
Width: 47'-0"
Depth: 41'-0"

Design by
©Select Home Designs

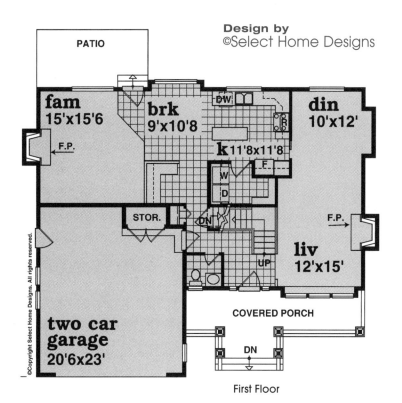

First Floor

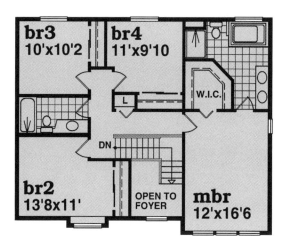

Second Floor

DESIGN HPT150097

First Floor: 1,113 sq. ft.
Second Floor: 835 sq. ft.
Total: 1,948 sq. ft.
Width: 54'-0"
Depth: 35'-8"

The covered porch on this charming two-story home provides a place to relax and enjoy peaceful summer evenings. A window high above the foyer brings light to this area, while the living room, dining room and open stairway work together to create an impressive entry. Warmed by the fireplace and lighted by a bay window and glass door, the rear of this home becomes a favorite gathering place for family activities. For convenience, a half-bath and laundry room are located near the kitchen, where a serving island and pantry provide a pleasant work area. The option of a third or fourth bedroom on the second floor is available with this plan. Choose the plan that best fits your family's needs and you will receive the same master bedroom suite with a luxurious bath and walk-in closet. A balcony overlooks the entry in both options, providing added excitement to this family-size home.

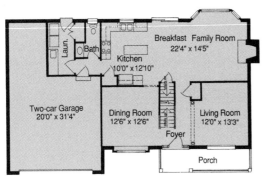

First Floor

Design by
©Studer Residential
Designs, Inc.

Second Floor

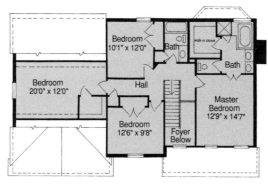

Optional Second Floor

Shingle siding and a covered front porch add style to this farmhouse design. The interior is arranged thoughtfully with an eye to varied lifestyles. Formal areas are on the left separated by columns: a living room with a tray ceiling, a fireplace and a formal dining room. A columned entry separates the two. The island kitchen connects directly to the breakfast room and the family room with fireplace. Note the double doors in the breakfast room to a rear covered porch. The second floor provides space for four bedrooms—one of them a master suite. The master bedroom has a vaulted ceiling and walk-in closet and features a luxurious bath with a separate tub and shower.

DESIGN HPT150098

First Floor: 1,092 sq. ft.
Second Floor: 1,147 sq. ft.
Total: 2,239 sq. ft.
Width: 47'-0"
Depth: 48'-0"

Design by
©Select Home Designs

First Floor

Second Floor

QUOTE ONE®

Cost to build? See page 182
to order complete cost estimate
to build this house in your area!

DESIGN HPT150099

First Floor: 1,012 sq. ft.
Second Floor: 1,140 sq. ft.
Total: 2,152 sq. ft.
Width: 48'-0"
Depth: 36'-4"

A charming combination of shingles and siding, this home also features keystone lintels, shutters and a columned entrance. The foyer leads to a two-story living room, complete with a fireplace and backyard views. The kitchen, on the right side of the plan, flows into the breakfast room, which opens to a sun deck. The left side of the plan is devoted to Bedroom 4, which accesses a hall bath. The second floor is home to the rest of the sleeping quarters. The master bedroom takes up the right side of the level, along with an accompanying full bath. Two additional bedrooms share a full bath.

Sundeck
12-0 x 10-0

Bdrm.4
11-0 x 10-0

Two Story Living Rm.
16-4 x 14-6

Brkfst.
10-0 x 11-4

Kit.
9-8 x 11-4

Bth.3

Foyer
7-2 x 11-10

Dining
10-8 x 12-10

Double Garage
19-4 x 21-8

Ref. Pant.

© 1999, Jannis Vann & Associates, Inc.

First Floor

Design by
©Jannis Vann &
Associates, Inc.

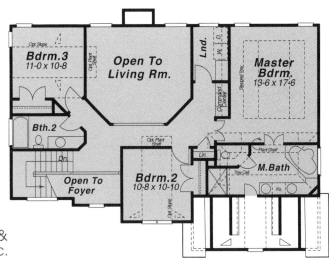

Bdrm.3
11-0 x 10-8

Open To Living Rm.

Lnd.

Master Bdrm.
13-6 x 17-6

Bth.2

Open To Foyer

Bdrm.2
10-8 x 10-10

M.Bath

Second Floor

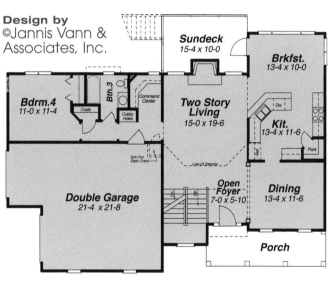

Sundeck
15-4 x 10-0

Brkfst.
13-4 x 10-0

Bdrm.4
11-0 x 11-4

Bth.3

Command
Center

Coats

Cubby
Holes

**Two Story
Living**
15-0 x 19-6

Kit.
13-4 x 11-6

W/H For
Slab/Crawl

Line Of Balcony

Pant.

Double Garage
21-4 x 21-8

**Open
Foyer**
7-0 x 5-10

Dining
13-4 x 11-6

Porch

First Floor

A mixture of stone, shakes and siding create interest for this charming two-story plan. The front porch with arched soffit is accented by the radius window with a flower box over the stairwell to the left. The foyer opens to the two-story living room. The U-shaped staircase helps to make this area seem expansive. To the rear, a glass-surrounded breakfast room opens to the kitchen overlooking the living room. The fireplace offers the option of a built-in TV cabinet above the fireplace. Nearby, a compact space features a built-in desk for the home computer and family record storage. A fourth bedroom and full bath are located on the ground floor, providing the perfect guest room or home office if need be.

DESIGN HPT150100

First Floor: 1,236 sq. ft.
Second Floor: 1,291 sq. ft.
Total: 2,527 sq. ft.
Width: 57'-0"
Depth: 41'-0"

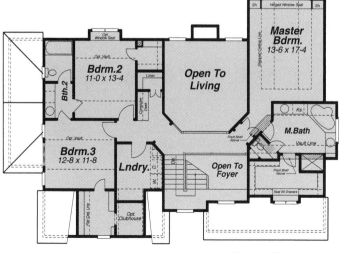

Sh. Hinged Window Seat Sh.

Opt.
Window Seat

**Master
Bdrm.**
13-6 x 17-4

Opt. Vault.

Bdrm.2
11-0 x 13-4

Bth.2

Linen

Computer
Desk

**Open To
Living**

Stepped Ceiling Line

Kn.

M.Bath

Vault Line

Opt. Vault.

Plant Shelf
Above

Bdrm.3
12-8 x 11-8

Lndry.

W. D.

**Open To
Foyer**

Plant Shelf
Above

Seat W/ Drawers

Flat Clg. Line

Opt.
Clubhouse

Second Floor

SHINGLE STYLE

DESIGN HPT150101

First Floor: 1,382 sq. ft.
Second Floor: 907 sq. ft.
Total: 2,289 sq. ft.
Width: 55'-0"
Depth: 42'-0"

Prominent eaves and a charming mixture of brick and shingle detailing are the distinguishing marks of this farmhouse. An open foyer leads you to a vaulted living area, complete with a fireplace for cold evenings. A cozy kitchen, pantry included, flows into a bayed breakfast area with a rear door to the sun deck. The first-floor master bedroom includes many amenities, including a full bath with plant shelves. A laundry room, command center and powder room complete the main level. Three additional bedrooms reside on the upper level, as do a full bath and unfinished storage space. The balcony opens to the living area and foyer below, creating a sense of spaciousness.

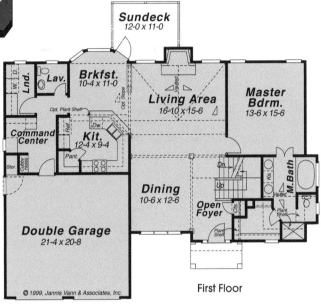

First Floor

© 1999, Jannis Vann & Associates, Inc.

Design by
©Jannis Vann & Associates, Inc.

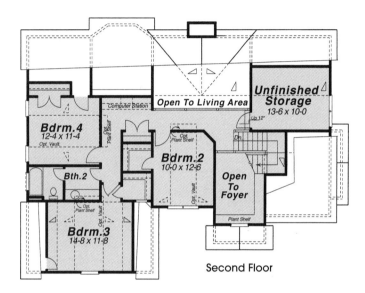

Second Floor

Brick detailing, shingles and siding come together to create a refined exterior on this country farmhouse. The foyer is flanked by a dining room and a living room/optional study. At the rear of the house, the two-story family room is graced with a central fireplace and rear-door access to a sun deck. The kitchen blends into the breakfast area and provides backyard views. Storage space, a powder room and a command center complete the first-floor of this plan. The sleeping quarters upstairs include a lavish master bedroom, with a full bath and sitting area, three vaulted family bedrooms, another full bath and a laundry area.

DESIGN HPT150102

First Floor: 1,160 sq. ft.
Second Floor: 1,316 sq. ft.
Total: 2,476 sq. ft.
Width: 52'-0"
Depth: 44'-0"

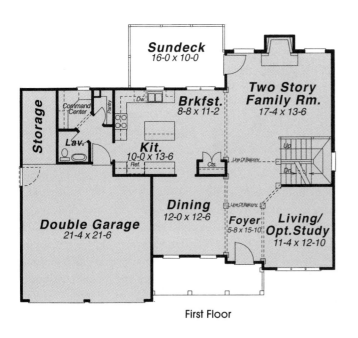

First Floor

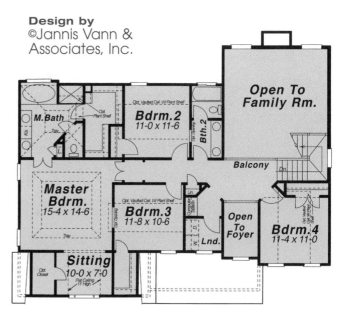

Design by
©Jannis Vann & Associates, Inc.

Second Floor

DESIGN HPT150103

First Floor: 1,771 sq. ft.
Second Floor: 1,235 sq. ft.
Total: 3,006 sq. ft.
Width: 61'-4"
Depth: 54'-0"

Design by
©Jannis Vann &
Associates, Inc.

Step into the two-story foyer, where a living room will greet you on the right and a boxed dining room on the left. Further into the plan is a two-story family room with a corner fireplace. The kitchen looks over a bar into the bayed breakfast area, which has rear-door access to the sun deck. The first-floor master bedroom is situated at the rear of the plan for maximum privacy and includes many lavish amenities. The second level presents many unique additions for the whole family. A future media space is perfect for a home theater or perhaps an additional bedroom. Three family bedrooms and two full baths complete the sleeping quarters. A storage space, a loft and overlooks to the two-story family room and foyer are included in this versatile design. Please specify basement, slab or crawlspace foundation when ordering.

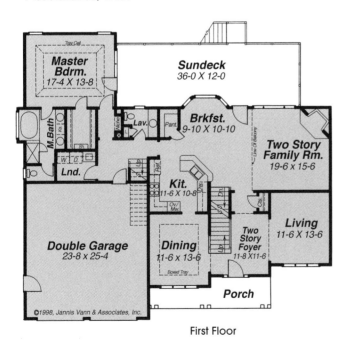

First Floor

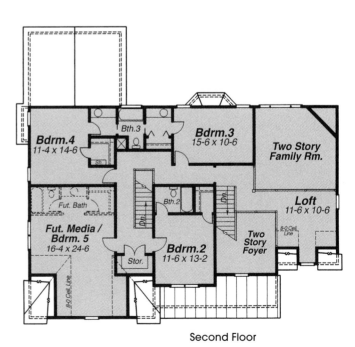

Second Floor

An elegant covered porch spans the front of this house and draws attention to the muntin windows and brick detailing. A two-story foyer is flanked by a dining room on the right and a living room on the left. A spacious kitchen—with plenty of counter space—leads into a cozy breakfast area, which opens to the rear sun deck. The two-story family room boasts a fireplace and an abundance of windows. A guest bedroom, with a full bath, completes the first level. A luxurious second-floor master bedroom includes a tray ceiling, sitting area, His and Hers walk-in closets and an amenity-filled bath. Three additional bedrooms, two full baths and a balcony overlook to the family room and foyer below round out this level.

DESIGN HPT150104

First Floor: 1,553 sq. ft.
Second Floor: 1,587 sq. ft.
Total: 3,140 sq. ft.
Width: 58'-0"
Depth: 41'-4"

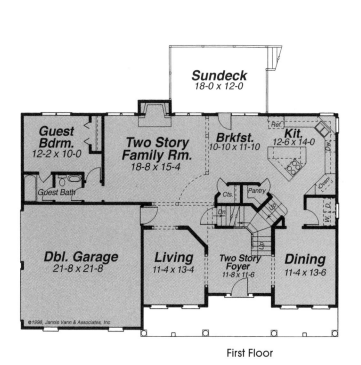

First Floor

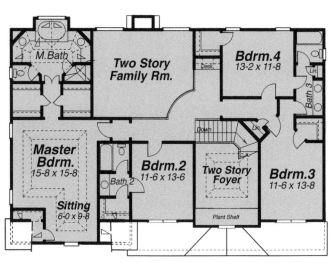

Second Floor

Design by
©Jannis Vann & Associates, Inc.

SHINGLE STYLE

DESIGN HPT150105

First Floor: 1,264 sq. ft.
Second Floor: 1,721 sq. ft.
Total: 2,985 sq. ft.
Width: 62'-4"
Depth: 50'-0"

Stacked stone, shakes and metal roofing create a warm, friendly exterior to this very traditional floor plan. The foyer features a curved staircase partially open to the second floor. Columns between decorative short walls divide the living room from the foyer. Columns also create a hallway to the breakfast room at the rear of the house. The breakfast room is glassed on three sides, making a sun-room feel. The spacious kitchen centers around the cooktop island and includes a pantry. Upstairs, four bedrooms complete the house. A second-floor laundry provides convenience, and the upper hall features a large computer desk to be shared by the whole family. The master suite has all the amenities—a tray ceiling, a sitting area and a walk-in closet easily big enough for two. Please specify basement, crawlspace or slab foundation when ordering.

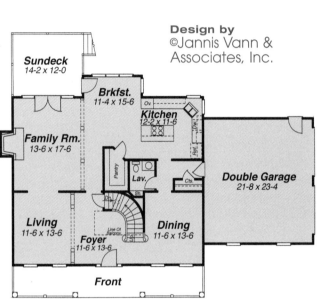

Design by
©Jannis Vann & Associates, Inc.

First Floor

Second Floor

The inviting country-style porch dominates this rambling plan. The two-story foyer looks through to a dramatic radius window on the staircase landing located on the rear wall of the house. The staircase separates the two-story family room from the breakfast room and kitchen. The laundry room, just behind a service porch, gives access to both the backyard as well as the stairs to the bonus room above the garage. An alcove entrance between the family room and living room features a built-in decorative niche. The optional entrance to the living room allows it to be used as an office or sitting room off the master suite. The master suite, located on the first floor, features a bay-window sitting area and a dramatic barrel ceiling in the full bath. Please specify basement, crawlspace or slab foundation when ordering.

DESIGN HPT150106

First Floor: 1,912 sq. ft.
Second Floor: 947 sq. ft.
Total: 2,859 sq. ft.
Bonus Room: 364 sq. ft.
Width: 86'-0"
Depth: 51'-0"

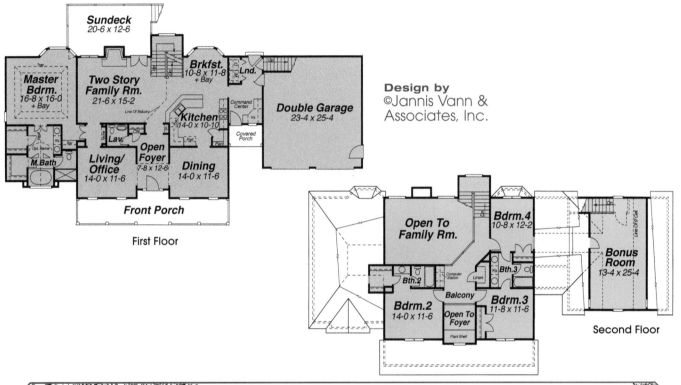

Design by
©Jannis Vann & Associates, Inc.

First Floor

Second Floor

DESIGN HPT150107

First Floor: 2,197 sq. ft.
Second Floor: 1,540 sq. ft.
Total: 3,737 sq. ft.
Bonus Room: 577 sq. ft.
Width: 81'-6"
Depth: 58'-0"

L

This sensational shingle home flirts with the future, while staying true to American traditional style. An elegant foyer opens to a spacious office or den—with French doors to the front covered porch—and leads back to casual living space for the family. A spacious gourmet kitchen adjoins the family room, which enjoys a cozy inglenook as well as access to the rear property. Each of the upstairs bedrooms includes a walk-in closet, special window treatment and private bath. The master suite features a bay window and French doors that open to an elegant bath with a tile-rimmed spa tub, twin lavatories with a knee-space vanity, glass-block shower and sizable walk-in closet. French doors open to bonus space that may be developed later.

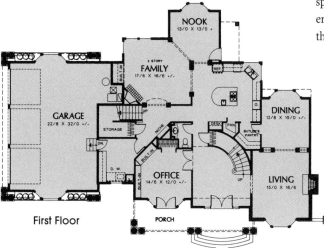

First Floor

Design by
©Alan Mascord Design
Associates, Inc.

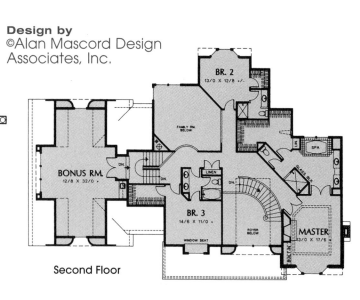

Second Floor

The blending of natural materials and a nostalgic farmhouse look gives this home its unique character. Inside, a sophisticated floor plan includes all the amenities demanded by today's upscale family. Three large covered porches—one on the front and two on the rear—provide outdoor entertaining areas. The kitchen features a built-in stone fireplace visible from the breakfast and sun rooms. The master suite includes a large sitting area and a luxurious bath. Upstairs, two additional bedrooms and a large game room will please family and guests. Please specify crawlspace or slab foundation when ordering.

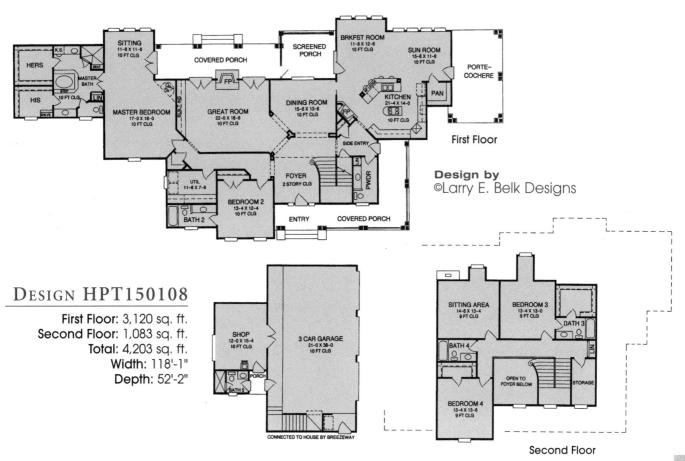

Design by
©Larry E. Belk Designs

DESIGN HPT150108

First Floor: 3,120 sq. ft.
Second Floor: 1,083 sq. ft.
Total: 4,203 sq. ft.
Width: 118'-1"
Depth: 52'-2"

SHINGLE STYLE

DESIGN HPT150109

First Floor: 1,333 sq. ft.
Second Floor: 1,158 sq. ft.
Total: 2,491 sq. ft.
Width: 68'-0"
Depth: 42'-6"

This two-story house is just the right home for a large family. The wraparound porch only adds to the charm of this home. This home features a well-laid-out floor plan with amenities that include a formal living room, formal dining room, inviting sun room and cozy family room. The oversized kitchen with a center island is great for meal planning. The nook is conveniently open to the kitchen, which flows directly into the family room, and is perfect for family conversations. The second floor includes a total of four bedrooms and an opening to the foyer. The large master bedroom features a full bath, which includes a whirlpool tub, walk-in shower and a roomy walk-in closet.

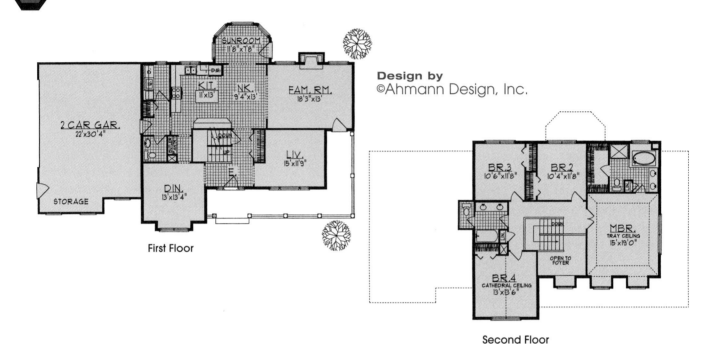

First Floor

Design by
©Ahmann Design, Inc.

Second Floor

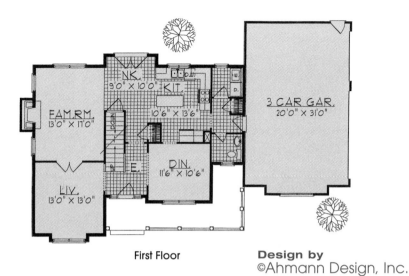

First Floor

Design by
©Ahmann Design, Inc.

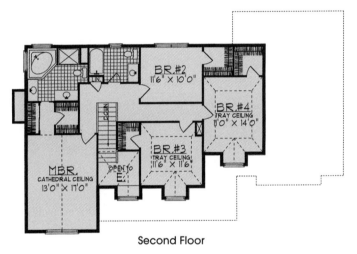

Second Floor

DESIGN HPT150110

First Floor: 1,065 sq. ft.
Second Floor: 1,171 sq. ft.
Total: 2,236 sq. ft.
Width: 60'-0"
Depth: 40'-0"

This welcoming two-story home offers the spaciousness you are looking for in a new home. The covered front porch leads to the foyer which invites guests into the living room. The formal living room is perfect for entertaining; or move through the French doors into the family room for around the fireplace. The formal dining room is available for special meals. The large open kitchen provides a center island and a sunny nook for breakfast and lunch. The master bedroom is your private retreat. Inside, you'll find a large walk-in closet and a private bath with two vanities, a corner spa tub and a shower. Three additional bedrooms share a full bath. Other amenities include a three-car garage, a main-floor laundry and a guest bath.

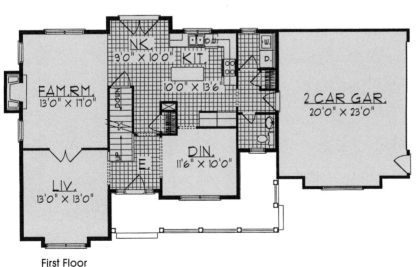

Second Floor

Design by
©Ahmann Design, Inc.

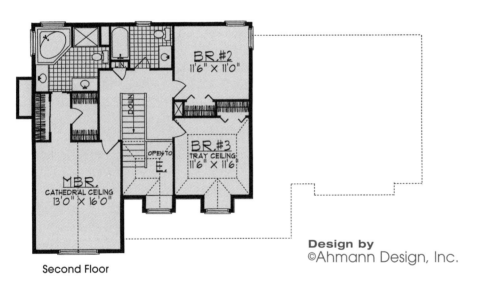

First Floor

DESIGN HPT150111

First Floor: 1,065 sq. ft.
Second Floor: 921 sq. ft.
Total: 1,986 sq. ft.
Width: 60'-0"
Depth: 34'-0"

Front-facing dormer windows, muntin and sunburst windows and a charming covered porch distinguish this home's exterior from others. On the left side of the plan, the living room accesses the family room through French doors. The family room is a perfect gathering place due to the central fireplace and accessibility to the kitchen. The island kitchen is nestled between a breakfast nook, with rear doors, and the dining area, which boasts front-yard views. Upstairs, a master bedroom features many amenities, including a cathedral ceiling, walk-in closet, garden tub and separate shower. Bedrooms 2 and 3 share a hall bath, while Bedroom 3 is graced with a tray ceiling and a dormer window.

The exterior of this home is truly one to behold with its second-floor flower box, shutters, prominent dormers, muntin windows and charming wood detailing set into the eaves. A spacious living room sits just off the foyer with French-door access to the rear covered patio. A dining room with a tray ceiling is also just off the foyer and is conveniently near the kitchen. The island kitchen offers an abundance of counter space and flows into a nook area and family room. A laundry room and pantry complete this kitchen area. A lavish first-floor master bedroom boasts His and Hers walk-in closets, a full bath and many other amenities. Bedroom 2 resides on the opposite end of the house and is graced with a full bath and a private porch. Bedrooms 3 and 4, two full baths and a game room occupy the second floor. Both the game room and Bedroom 4 share a balcony.

DESIGN HPT150112

First Floor: 2,390 sq. ft.
Second Floor: 1,042 sq. ft.
Total: 3,432 sq. ft.
Width: 70'-0"
Depth: 76'-4"

Design by
©Home Design
Services, Inc.

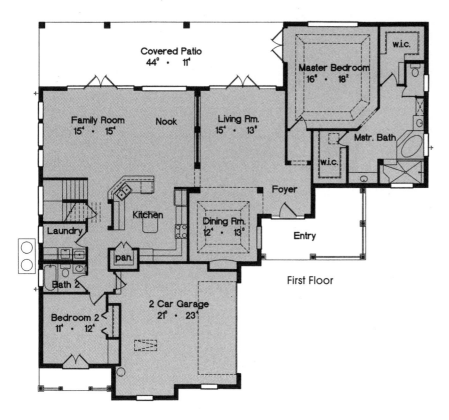

First Floor

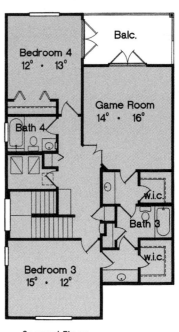

Second Floor

SHINGLE STYLE

DESIGN HPT150113

First Floor: 1,650 sq. ft.
Second Floor: 1,325 sq. ft.
Total: 2,975 sq. ft.
Width: 57'-7"
Depth: 53'-4"

This home has all the modern conveniences a family would desire, plus many amenities that enhance this plan. Double doors open to the foyer flanked by a library—complete with bay window—and a tray-ceilinged dining room. The great room is enhanced with a fireplace and built-in bookshelves. The island kitchen provides plenty of counter space and is situated near a bayed breakfast area, perfect for taking in the backyard sights. A roomy laundry area and computer center is positioned on the right side of the plan, as is the two-car garage. The second floor holds the master bedroom, two family bedrooms, two full baths and a hall that looks to the foyer below.

Design by
©Studer Residential
Designs, Inc.

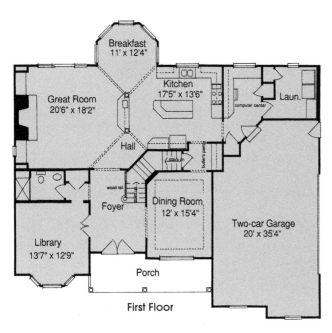

First Floor

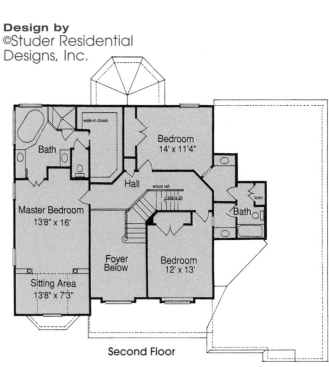

Second Floor

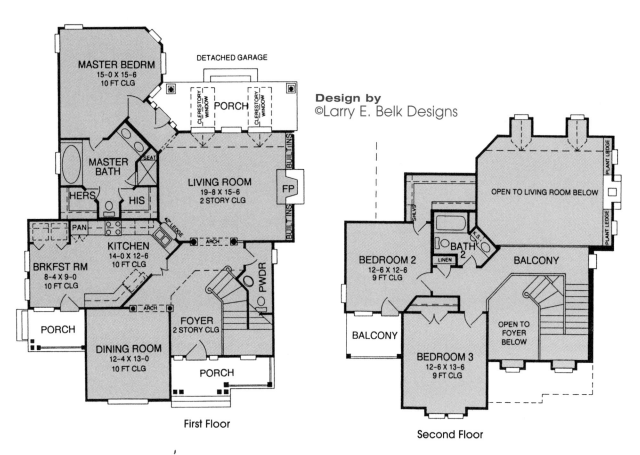

A charming elevation gives this home its curbside appeal. Inside, the two-story foyer opens through archways to the living and dining rooms. Clerestory windows flood the living room with natural light. The kitchen and breakfast room are nearby. An angled sink, with a serving ledge and pass-through, opens the kitchen to the living room beyond. An old-time side porch off the kitchen enhances the look of the home and provides convenient access to the outside. The master bath has all the frills and includes roomy His and Hers walk-in closets. Two bedrooms and a bath are located upstairs. A lovely balcony is located off Bedroom 2. This plan includes a two-car detached garage. Please specify crawlspace or slab foundation when ordering.

DESIGN HPT150114

First Floor: 1,482 sq. ft.
Second Floor: 631 sq. ft.
Total: 2,113 sq. ft.
Width: 41'-10"
Depth: 56'-5"

Design by
©Larry E. Belk Designs

First Floor

Second Floor

Design by
Donald A. Gardner
Architects, Inc.

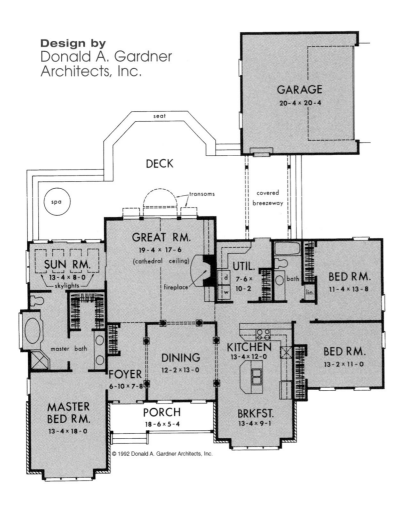

GARAGE
20-4 × 20-4

seat

DECK

spa

covered
breezeway

transoms

GREAT RM.
19-4 × 17-6
(cathedral ceiling)

fireplace

SUN RM.
13-4 × 8-0
skylights

UTIL.
7-6 ×
10-2

d

w

bath

lin.

BED RM.
11-4 × 13-8

master bath

KITCHEN
13-4 × 12-0

DINING
12-2 × 13-0

FOYER
6-10 × 7-8

BED RM.
13-2 × 11-0

MASTER
BED RM.
13-4 × 18-0

PORCH
18-6 × 5-4

BRKFST.
13-4 × 9-1

© 1992 Donald A. Gardner Architects, Inc.

DESIGN HPT150115

Square Footage: 2,112
Width: 65'-0"
Depth: 76'-1"

Indoor/outdoor relationships are given close attention in this plan. Windows on all sides, including dormers in the front and transoms in the great room, let in the view, while sliding glass doors in the sun room and great room provide access to a spacious deck. Box-bay windows enliven the master bedroom and breakfast area. Other highlights include columns setting off the dining room, and a fireplace and cathedral ceiling in the great room. Two family bedrooms share a full bath. The master bedroom, located on the left side of the plan for privacy, boasts a walk-in closet, twin-basin vanity, garden tub and separate shower.

This one-story Victorian farmhouse features a covered porch, Palladian windows and decorative fish-scale shingles. A large kitchen and breakfast area provide plenty of room to maneuver for the cook of the family. A cathedral ceiling graces the spacious living room. The master bedroom is located on the right side of the plan, and includes a cathedral ceiling in the bath, plant ledges and a private covered patio. On the left side, three additional bedrooms share a full bath. A large utility area furnishes convenience and economy.

DESIGN HPT150116

Square Footage: 2,495
Width: 87'-10"
Depth: 62'-7"

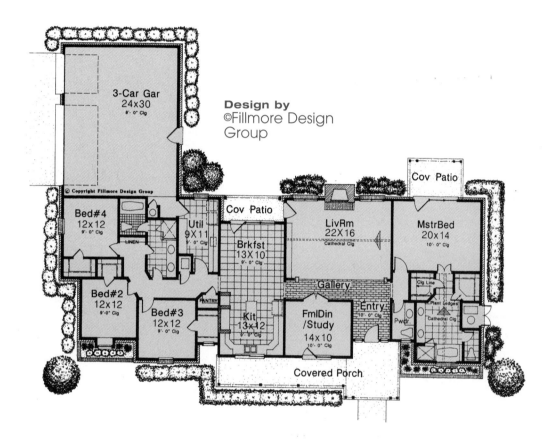

Design by
©Fillmore Design Group

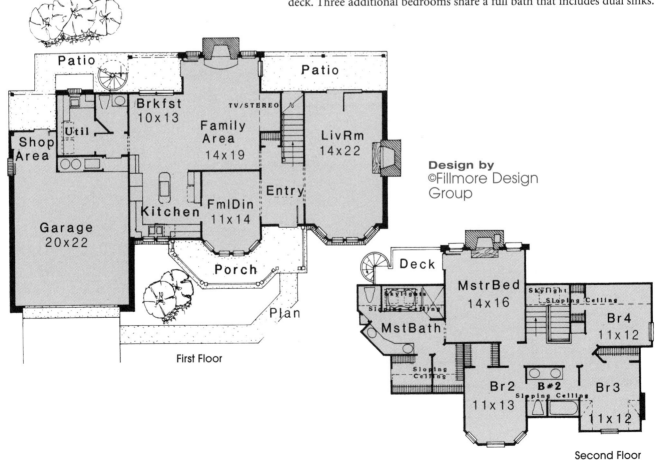

DESIGN HPT150117

First Floor: 1,304 sq. ft.
Second Floor: 1,064 sq. ft.
Total: 2,368 sq. ft.
Width: 65'-0"
Depth: 41'-10"

This Prairie-style home features slight Victorian detailing and a covered front porch that is ideal for lazy Sunday afternoons. The living room includes a fireplace and a bay window that provides a front view. The dining room easily accesses the kitchen, allowing for convenient serving and entertaining. The sleeping quarters reside upstairs. The master bedroom is enhanced with a sloped ceiling, skylights, a fireplace and access to a private deck. Three additional bedrooms share a full bath that includes dual sinks.

Design by
©Fillmore Design Group

Patio

Brkfst
10 x 13

Util

TV/STEREO

Family Area
14 x 19

Patio

LivRm
14 x 22

Shop Area

Kitchen

FmlDin
11 x 14

Entry

Garage
20 x 22

Porch

Plan

First Floor

Deck

MstrBed
14 x 16

Skylight

Sloping Ceiling

MstBath

Br 4
11 x 12

Skylight

Sloping Ceiling

Br 2
11 x 13

B #2

Sloping Ceiling

Br 3
11 x 12

Sloping Ceiling

Second Floor

This large Victorian two-story home displays brick-and-shingle siding and boasts two unique bay windows with conical roofs and a covered porch. The expansive kitchen and country kitchen areas look to the rear patio, as does the family room, complete with a fireplace and wet bar. The master bedroom accesses a private wood deck and is enhanced with two large walk-in closets, as well as a jacuzzi-style tub. Two separate staircases lead upstairs to the sleeping quarters. Three bedrooms reside on the second floor and share a full bath and a wood deck. A balcony looks down to the entry below.

DESIGN HPT150118

First Floor: 3,073 sq. ft.
Second Floor: 1,230 sq. ft.
Total: 4,303 sq. ft.
Width: 101'-7"
Depth: 52'-5"

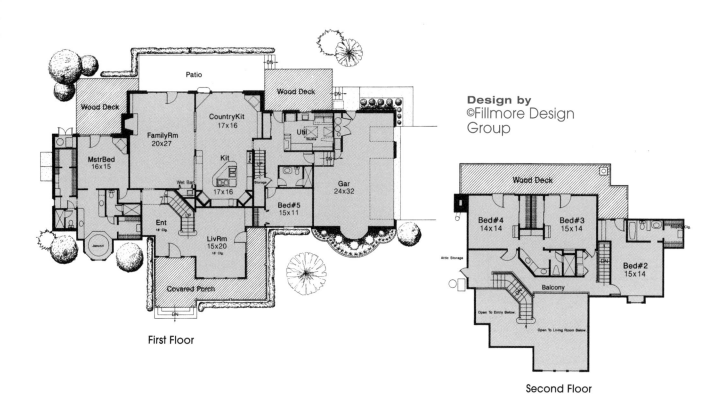

Design by
©Fillmore Design Group

First Floor

Second Floor

SHINGLE STYLE

Design by
©Larry W. Garnett &
Associates, Inc.

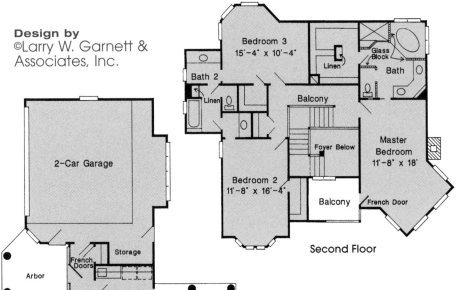

Second Floor

First Floor

DESIGN HPT150119

First Floor: 1,401 sq. ft.
Second Floor: 1,189 sq. ft.
Total: 2,590 sq. ft.
Width: 44'-8"
Depth: 75'-4"

The double leaded-glass doors of this Shingle-style design open into an elegant foyer. The study features raised-panel walls, built-in bookcases and a fireplace. Overlooking the breakfast area and the living room is a spacious kitchen with a walk-in pantry and island cooktop. The living room contains a built-in media center, French doors to the rear porch and a refreshment bar. Upstairs, the secluded master suite offers a windowed alcove and access to the covered front balcony. The elegant bath utilizes glass-block walls for the shower and water closet areas. A corner garden tub and a large walk-in closet complete this area. The additional bedrooms each have unique bay windows and private lavatories.

Design HPT150120

First Floor: 1,637 sq. ft.
Second Floor: 1,062 sq. ft.
Total: 2,699 sq. ft.
Width: 49'-6"
Depth: 75'-0"

Designed to maximize views to the front, side and rear outdoor areas, this home utilizes strategically placed windows and an open floor plan. The two-way fireplace and half-wall with built-in bookcases separate the living and dining areas. A center work island and walk-in pantry, along with a built-in breakfast nook, are special kitchen amenities. The master suite provides a comfortable retreat with a bay-windowed sitting area and a magnificent bath. Upstairs, a large balcony with a window seat leads to three additional bedrooms. Bedrooms 3 and 4 each feature built-in desks and private dressing areas. Bedroom 2 has a private bath, built-in desk and French door opening to a rear deck.

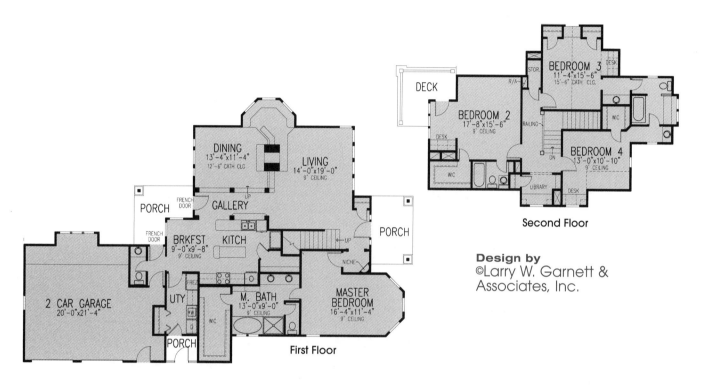

First Floor

Second Floor

Design by
©Larry W. Garnett & Associates, Inc.

The leaded-glass front door opens to a spacious foyer, which offers a view of the formal dining room. A library alcove, with windows above a desk and a bookcase below the stairs, connects the living and family areas. The kitchen features an island cooktop, an angled window and sink and a French door leading to the side veranda. Adjacent to the kitchen is a staircase to an optional game room or living quarters. The master suite contains a private media center with built-in seating and cabinets for audio and video equipment. The two additional bedrooms each feature a private bathroom.

DESIGN HPT150121

First Floor: 1,353 sq. ft.
Second Floor: 1,279 sq. ft.
Total: 2,632 sq. ft.
Width: 55'-6"
Depth: 66'-8"

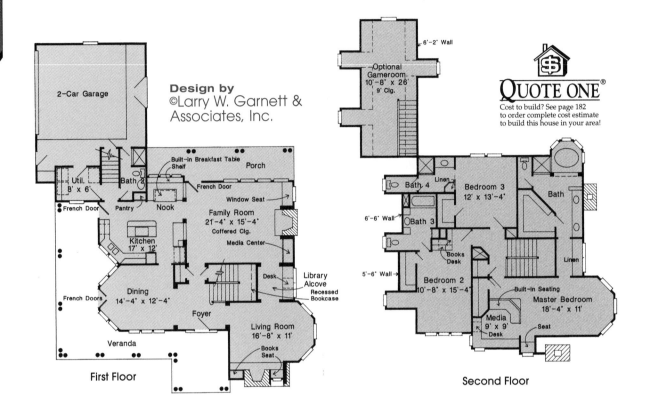

Design by
©Larry W. Garnett &
Associates, Inc.

QUOTE ONE®
Cost to build? See page 182
to order complete cost estimate
to build this house in your area!

First Floor

Second Floor

First Floor

Future Bonus Rm.
33⁸ · 12²

2 Car Garage
33⁸ · 22²

Covered Patio

Grand Room
19⁵ · 20⁴

Nook

Kitchen

Laundry

Dining Rm.
12⁵ · 14⁵

Master Bedroom
20⁴ · 13³

Mstr. Bath

Pwdr.

w.i.c.

w.i.c.

Home Office
14⁴ · 12³

Entry   Foyer

Covered Patio

DOWN

Loft

Mech.

w.i.c.

w.i.c.

Bedroom 2
12⁴ · 15⁵

Bedroom 3
12⁴ · 14⁵

Bath 2

Second Floor

Attic/Storage
22² · 12²

Third Floor

Design by
©Home Design
Services, Inc.

DESIGN HPT150122

First Floor: 2,376 sq. ft.
Second Floor: 1,078 sq. ft.
Total: 3,454 sq. ft.
Bonus Room: 549 sq. ft.
Width: 80'-6"
Depth: 85'-6"

An abundance of muntin windows and a shingle facade are the defining characteristics of this design. A covered porch leads into a dining room that is graced with French doors to the front porch. A home office, complete with a convenient powder room, flanks the foyer on the right. The master bedroom, also on the right side of the plan, boasts a full bath, His and Hers walk-in closets and French-door access to the rear covered porch. The grand room flows into the nook and kitchen. The second level holds two family bedrooms—each with their own walk-in closet—that share a lavish walk-through bath. A large future bonus room and a loft complete this level. The third floor houses a spacious attic/storage room, perfect for all the odds and ends of a busy family.

Towards the end of the Victorian era, a new style began to emerge along the Eastern Seabord. Later referred to as the Shingle style, these new designs were influenced by the Colonial Revival and Queen Anne homes. Often incorporating diverse architectural elements, shingle siding is one of the common elements of this style. With its cantilevered gable sloping in a gentle curve to the first floor and a raised turret, this design is representative of this late 19th-Century style. Besides the living and dining rooms with coffered ceilings, the home boasts a study with curved walls, a central gallery and a family room with a sunken media center. The island kitchen has an adjacent breakfast booth. Upstairs are a grand master suite and three additional bedrooms.

DESIGN HPT150123

First Floor: 1,812 sq. ft.
Second Floor: 1,997 sq. ft.
Total: 3,809 sq. ft.
Width: 49'-2"
Depth: 71'-8"

Design by
©Larry W. Garnett & Associates, Inc.

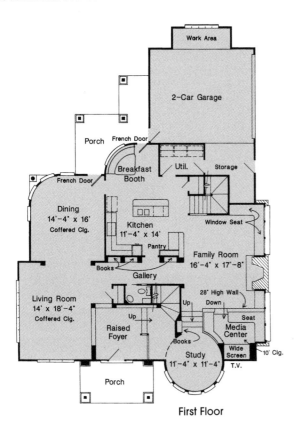

First Floor

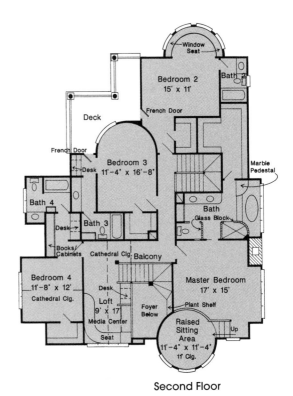

Second Floor

R eminiscent of the fashionable summer homes of Newport and Cape Cod, this home typifies the Shingle style with its wide verandas, shingled surfaces, Palladian window and circular tower. The library features a built-in bookcase and circular study. To the left of the fireplace in the game room, a brick archway houses a built-in media center. To the right, a matching brick archway leads to the adjoining pub and walk-in wet bar. Windows surround the spacious kitchen. The second-floor master suite includes two oversized walk-in closets and a luxury bath. Three additional bedrooms and two baths, as well as a multi-purpose media room, are also on the second floor. Plans for a three-car detached garage with second-floor living quarters are included.

DESIGN HPT150124

First Floor: 2,083 sq. ft.
Second Floor: 1,938 sq. ft.
Total: 4,021 sq. ft.
Width: 65'-4"
Depth: 56'-0"

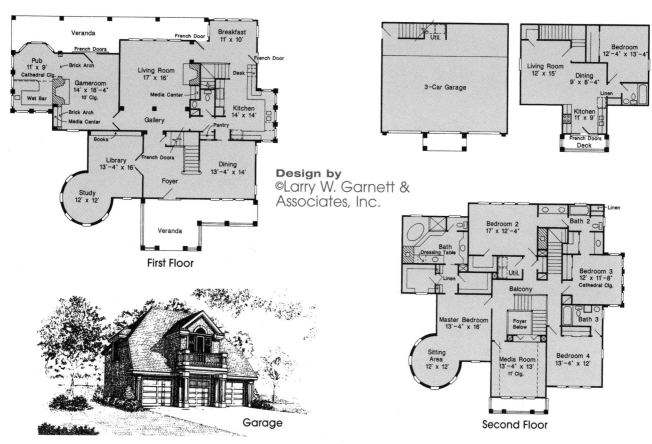

Design by
©Larry W. Garnett & Associates, Inc.

First Floor

Garage

Second Floor

DESIGN HPT150125

First Floor: 1,399 sq. ft.
Second Floor: 1,123 sq. ft.
Total: 2,522 sq. ft.
Width: 57'-6"
Depth: 46'-0"

L D

Design by
©Home Planners

Classic Victorian styling comes to the forefront in this Queen Anne two-story home. Complementary fish-scale-adorned pediments top the bayed tower to the left and the garage to the right. Smaller versions are found at the dormer windows above a spindlework porch. The interior boasts comfortable living quarters for the entire family. The formal living and dining rooms sit on opposite sides of the wide foyer. To the rear, a bay-windowed family kitchen is warmed by a fireplace. A small library with its own fireplace shares a covered porch with the informal gathering area. Three bedrooms on the second floor include a master suite with a grand bath.

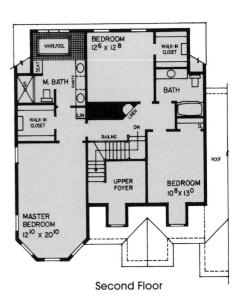

Second Floor

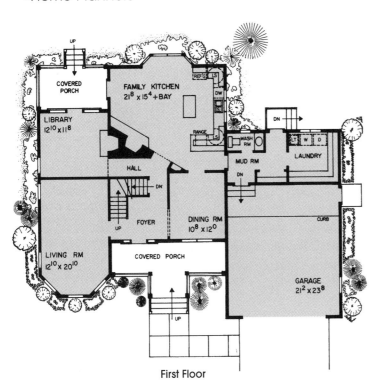

First Floor

QUOTE ONE®

Cost to build? See page 182
to order complete cost estimate
to build this house in your area!

A covered porch and Victorian accents create a classical elevation. Double doors to the entry open to a spacious great room and an elegant dining room. In the gourmet kitchen, features include an island snack bar and a large pantry. French doors lead to the breakfast area, which also enjoys access to a covered porch. Cathedral ceilings in the master bedroom and dressing area add an exquisite touch. His and Hers walk-in closets, a large dressing area with dual sinks and a whirlpool tub complement the private bath. A vaulted ceiling in Bedroom 2 accents a window seat and an arched transom window.

DESIGN HPT150126

First Floor: 905 sq. ft.
Second Floor: 863 sq. ft.
Total: 1,768 sq. ft.
Width: 40'-8"
Depth: 46'-0"

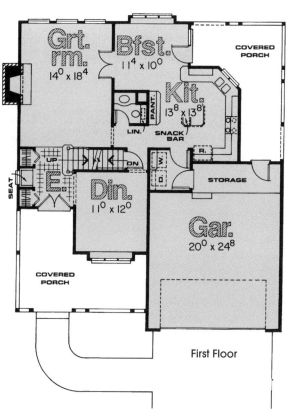

First Floor

Design by
©Design Basics, Inc.

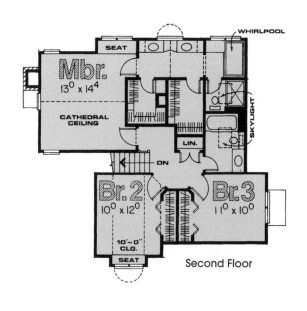

Second Floor

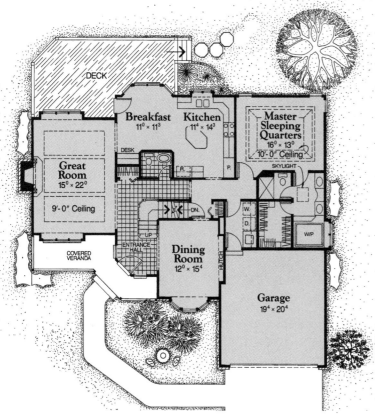

DECK

Breakfast
11⁰ × 11³

Kitchen
11⁴ × 14³

Master
Sleeping
Quarters
16⁰ × 13⁰
10'-0" Ceiling

SKYLIGHT

Great
Room
15⁰ × 22⁰

9'-0" Ceiling

DESK

R.

P.

DN.

UP

W.
D.

W/P

COVERED
VERANDA

ENTRANCE
HALL

HUTCH

Dining
Room
12⁰ × 15⁴

Garage
19⁴ × 20⁴

First Floor

DESIGN HPT150127

First Floor: 1,553 sq. ft.
Second Floor: 725 sq. ft.
Total: 2,278 sq. ft.
Width: 54'-0"
Depth: 50'-0"

The intricate detailing, tall brick chimney and stately veranda on the elevation of this four-bedroom, 1½-story home blend effortlessly into Victorian elegance. Other preferred features include: the two-story entrance hall, a bay window in the formal dining room, the open island kitchen with a pantry and desk, and the private master suite with vaulted ceiling and two-person whirlpool tub in the master bath. This versatile plan is designed for practical living with guest rooms or children's bedrooms located on the upper level. One of these second-story bedrooms features a walk-in closet.

Design by
©Design Basics, Inc.

Sleeping
Quarters
11⁶ × 11¹⁰

Sleeping
Quarters
11⁶ × 11¹⁰

LINEN

DN.

CLOTHES
CHUTE

OPEN TO
BELOW

Sleeping
Quarters
11⁰ × 11⁶

TRANS.

Second Floor

DESIGN HPT150128

First Floor: 1,120 sq. ft.
Second Floor: 1,411 sq. ft.
Total: 2,531 sq. ft.
Width: 57'-4"
Depth: 33'-0"

Victorian detailing lends this four-bedroom home eye-catching charm, with fish-scale shingles, pinnacles and gingerbread decorations on the gables. To the left of the entry, a formal dining room provides space for a hutch. Across the entry, the living room's double doors open to the family room and its warming fireplace. Sharing the open space with the living room are a bay-windowed breakfast nook and kitchen. This kitchen will please any cook, with an island workstation, pantry and window over the sink. Tucked upstairs, away from everyday noises, four bedrooms all include walk-in closets. The master bedroom is complete with a tray ceiling, whirlpool bath, shower, dual vanity sinks and compartmented toilet.

Kit.
9⁸ x 10⁶

Bfst.
9⁸ x 12⁶

Fam. Rm.
16⁰ x 17⁰

Gar.
21⁰ x 24⁸

R.

PANTRY

DN

D. W.

HUTCH SPACE

Din. Rm.
12⁰ x 11⁰

UP

E.

Liv. Rm.
12⁰ x 13⁰

COVERED PORCH

Design by
©Design Basics, Inc.

First Floor

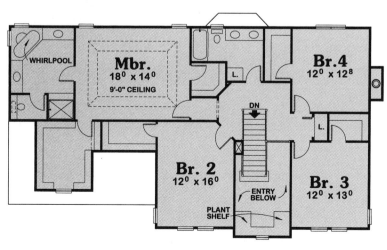

WHIRLPOOL

Mbr.
18⁰ x 14⁰
9'-0" CEILING

Br.4
12⁰ x 12⁸

L.

DN

L.

Br. 2
12⁰ x 16⁰

ENTRY BELOW

PLANT SHELF

Br. 3
12⁰ x 13⁰

Second Floor

SHINGLE STYLE

DESIGN HPT150129

First Floor: 1,474 sq. ft.
Second Floor: 1,554 sq. ft.
Total: 3,028 sq. ft.
Bonus Room: 436 sq. ft.
Width: 76'-8"
Depth: 52'-8"

The exterior of this home is sure to get attention with a Victorian turret and its ribbon of windows. The three-car garage, a tiled powder room, utility room and kitchen take up the left side of the plan. Inside the kitchen, a cooktop island and plenty of counter space provide room for meal preparation. In the family room—located near the entrance to the office—is a built-in media center and an optional fireplace. Four bedrooms, three full baths and a vaulted family room occupy the second floor. The French doors open to the master bedroom where the fireplace and private balcony satisfy a high standard of living. Located between Bedrooms 2 and 3, a compartmented bath sports a double-bowl vanity. Bedroom 4 holds an angled entry and access to the third bath. Please specify basement or slab foundation when ordering.

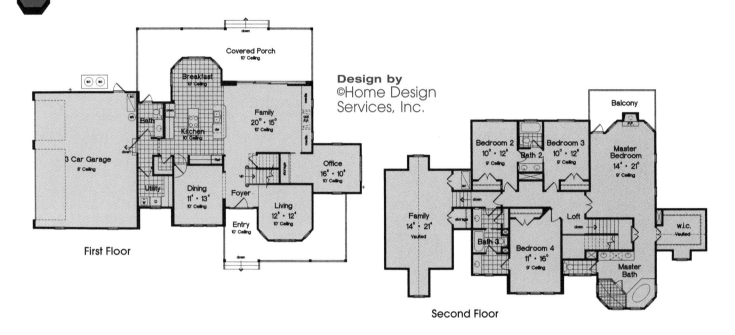

Design by
©Home Design
Services, Inc.

First Floor

Second Floor

Two turrets, scalloped shingles and gingerbread trim enhance this majestic Queen Anne design. A welcoming covered porch gives way to the foyer, which is flanked by an expansive living/dining area and a den that doubles as a study. The galley-style kitchen offers an island work counter and adjoins a breakfast bay that opens to a screened patio. Sleeping quarters are thoughtfully placed upstairs, away from the main living area. An indulgent master bedroom features a sitting area, a fireplace and a full bath encircled by a turret. Three additional bedrooms, two with walk-in closets, share a second full bath.

DESIGN HPT150130

First Floor: 1,379 sq. ft.
Second Floor: 1,304 sq. ft.
Total: 2,683 sq. ft.
Width: 54'-8"
Depth: 61'-4"

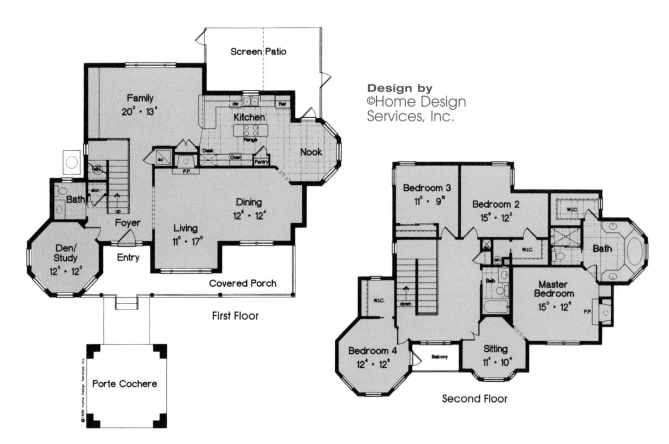

Design by
©Home Design Services, Inc.

First Floor

Second Floor

DESIGN HPT150131

First Floor: 2,083 sq. ft.
Second Floor: 1,013 sq. ft.
Total: 3,096 sq. ft.
Width: 74'-0"
Depth: 88'-0"

This beautiful design is accented by the circular front porch and the abundance of windows. The entry leads into a grand foyer, where a radius staircase presents itself. Most of the rooms in this house are graced with tray, stepped or vaulted ceilings, adding a sense of spaciousness to the plan. The first-floor master suite boasts many amenities, including a private lanai, His and Hers walk-in closets, a bayed tub area and a separate shower. Other unique features on the first floor include a study, with a window seat and built-in cabinetry, a breakfast nook, butler's pantry, utility room and outdoor kitchen, amongst others. The second floor houses three family bedrooms and two full baths. Bedroom 3 boasts an octagonal ceiling, while the ceiling of Bedroom 2 is vaulted. A computer center, linen area and loft complete the second floor.

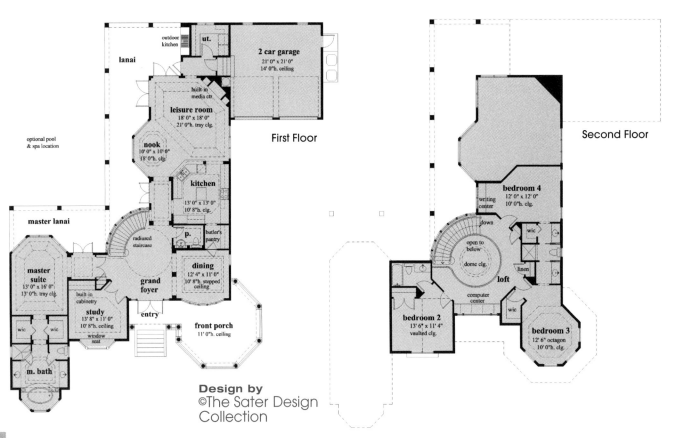

Design by
©The Sater Design
Collection

COASTAL CREATIONS

Vacation and waterfront homes

DESIGN HPT150132

First Floor: 784 sq. ft.
Second Floor: 275 sq. ft.
Total: 1,059 sq. ft.
Width: 32'-0"
Depth: 30'-0"

L D

This chalet-type vacation home, with its steep, overhanging roof, will catch the eye of even the most casual onlooker. It is designed to be completely livable whether it's the season for swimming or skiing. The dormitory on the upper level will sleep many vacationers, while the two bedrooms on the first floor provide the more convenient and conventional sleeping facilities. The upper level overlooks the beam-ceilinged living and dining area. With a wraparound terrace and plenty of storage space, this is a perfect design.

Design by
©Home Planners

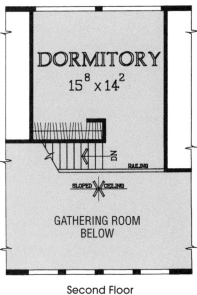

QUOTE ONE®
Cost to build? See page 182
to order complete cost estimate
to build this house in your area!

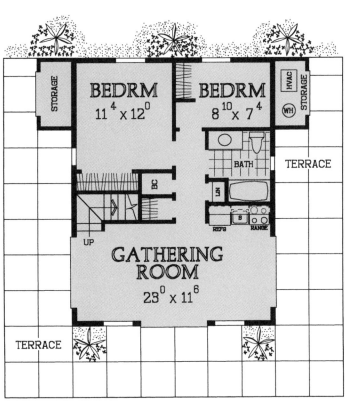

STORAGE

BEDRM
11⁴ x 12⁰

BEDRM
8¹⁰ x 7⁴

HVAC

STORAGE

WH

BATH

TERRACE

BC

UP

GATHERING
ROOM
23⁰ x 11⁶

REFG RANGE

TERRACE

First Floor

DORMITORY
15⁸ x 14²

DN

RAILING

SLOPED CEILING

GATHERING ROOM
BELOW

Second Floor

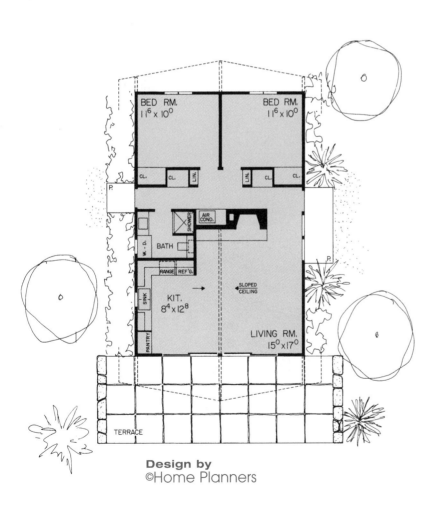

BED RM.
11⁶ x 10⁰

BED RM.
11⁶ x 10⁰

CL.   CL.   LIN.   LIN.   CL.   CL.

P.

SHOWER   AIR COND.

BATH

W. D.

RANGE   REF'G.

SINK

SLOPED CEILING

KIT.
8⁴ x 12⁸

PANTRY

P.

LIVING RM.
15⁰ x 17⁰

TERRACE

Design by
©Home Planners

DESIGN HPT150133

Square Footage: 864
Width: 34'-8"
Depth: 48'-0"

A true vacationer's delight, this two-bedroom home extends the finest contemporary livability. Two sets of sliding glass doors open off the kitchen and living room where a sloped ceiling lends added dimension. In the kitchen, full counter space and cabinetry assure ease in meal preparation. A pantry stores all of your canned and boxed goods. In the living room, a fireplace serves as a relaxing as well as a practical feature. The rear of the plan is comprised of two bedrooms of identical size. A nearby full bath holds a washer/dryer unit. Two additional closets, as well as two linen closets, add to storage capabilities.

DESIGN HPT150134

Square Footage: 1,312
Width: 40'-0"
Depth: 60'-0"

BED RM.
11⁰ x 10⁰

BUNK RM.
6⁴ x 10⁰

BUNK RM.
6⁴ x 10⁰

BED RM.
11⁰ x 10⁰

CHEST

CHEST

CL.

CL.

CL.

CL.

BATH

BATH

AIR COND

W. B. D.

CL.

CL.

RANGE

S.

REF.

KIT.

STOR. CABS.

SNACK BAR

DINING

PREFAB FIREPLACE

SLOPING CEILING

LIVING
23⁴ x 32⁰

DECK

Design by
©Home Planners

Here is a wonderfully organized plan with an architectural design that commands attention, both inside and out. The dramatic rooflines, pointed glass and gable-end walls bring the outdoors in with beautiful views. The delightful deck echoes the roofline and invites outdoor entertainment. Inside, the spacious living room is crowned by a sloping ceiling with an exposed ridge beam. A free-standing fireplace will make its contribution to a cheerful atmosphere. The sleeping zone has two bedrooms, two bunk rooms, two full baths, two built-in chests and lots of closet space.

This home is enhanced with the intricate details of fish-scale shingles and a prominent bay window. The foyer leads into the living room, complete with a fireplace, bay window and sloped ceiling. A railing separates this room from the dining room, which sports a door to the rear deck/patio. The island kitchen is enhanced with a pantry, desk, an abundance of counter space and easy access to the breakfast room. A laundry room and plenty of coat closets add convenience to the lower level. The second level is home to the sleeping quarters, with the master bedroom and full bath dominating the right side. Bedrooms 2 and 3 share a walk-through full bath.

DESIGN HPT150135

First Floor: 1,100 sq. ft.
Second Floor: 1,007 sq. ft.
Total: 2,107 sq. ft.
Width: 51'-0"
Depth: 39'-4"

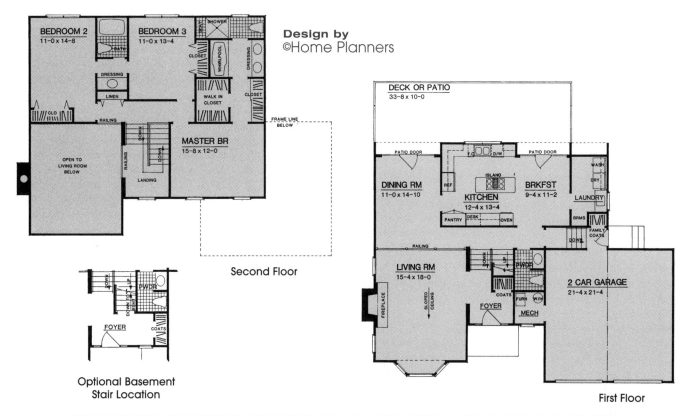

Design by
©Home Planners

Second Floor

Optional Basement
Stair Location

First Floor

DESIGN HPT150136

First Floor: 1,180 sq. ft.
Second Floor: 528 sq. ft.
Total: 1,708 sq. ft.
Width: 41'-4"
Depth: 45'-0"

With a combination of shingles and flagstone detailing, this country home is perfect for a rustic setting. A spacious porch leads into the foyer, where a uniquely placed kitchen is at its right. The kitchen leads to a laundry area and a convenient powder room. The two-story casual dining area and great room are combined for a snug atmosphere and share a fireplace. The master bedroom boasts a sitting area, which opens to the rear porch, large walk-in closet, dual basins and a compartmented toilet. The second level is home to two family bedrooms which share a hall bath. Attic storage is available and a balcony overlook to the great room below is also provided.

Design by
©Garden Houses of the 1920s, LLC

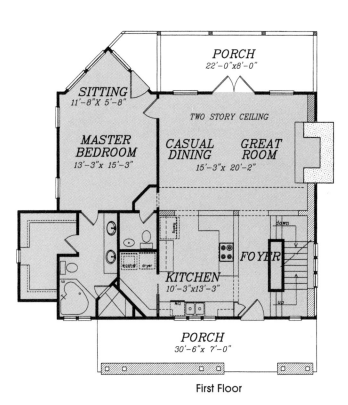

First Floor

Second Floor

T his home is marked by interesting angles, two chimneys and rustic brick detailing. French doors open to a foyer that is flanked by a well-lit formal dining room on the left and a hearth-warmed study on the right. The expansive great room also sports a fireplace, as well as a vaulted ceiling and French doors that open to the rear property. The great room flows into the spacious island kitchen, which leads to a breakfast area with an abundance of windows. The second level is home to the sleeping quarters. The master suite is enhanced with a sitting area, tray ceiling and large full bath. Bedrooms 2 and 3 are also large, each with their own walk-in closet and full bath. Bedroom 2 is highlighted with a dormer window for front-property views.

DESIGN HPT150137

First Floor: 1,530 sq. ft.
Second Floor: 1,363 sq. ft.
Total: 4,423 sq. ft.
Width: 36'-0"
Depth: 60'-0"

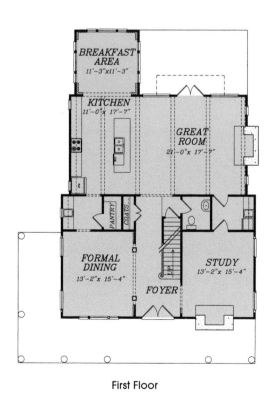

First Floor

Design by
©Garden Houses of
the 1920s, LLC

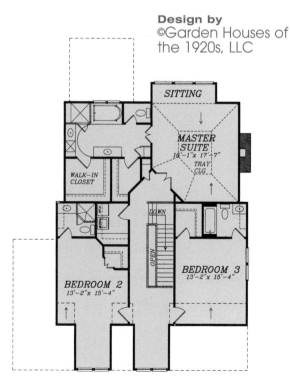

Second Floor

DESIGN HPT150138

SHINGLE STYLE

First Floor: 1,825 sq. ft.
Second Floor: 1,020 sq. ft.
Total: 3,661 sq. ft.
Width: 49'-8"
Depth: 57'-0"

A flagstone-decorated covered porch opens through French doors to a foyer where stone walls lead into the casual dining/great room area. This room is graced with a two-story ceiling and fireplace, as well as three sets of French doors opening to the rear porch. The kitchen leads into the breakfast area, which provides a door to the laundry room. The master bedroom includes a sitting area, walk-in closet, linen area and many other luxuries. Spacious family bedrooms share a full bath. A large loft is provided for a play area, bookshelves or whatever you desire. A balcony overlook allows views to the great room below, creating a sense of spaciousness.

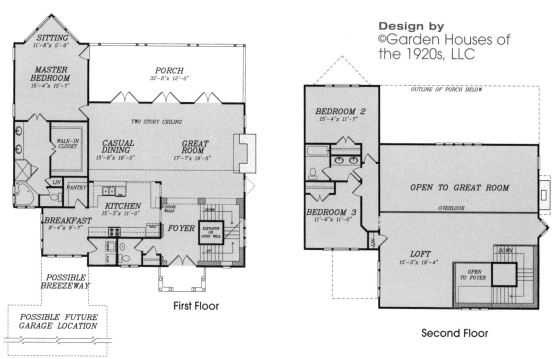

Design by
©Garden Houses of the 1920s, LLC

First Floor

Second Floor

This compact home displays a prominent chimney, a wealth of windows and shingle detailing. A cozy living room presents itself upon entry and is graced with a fireplace and charming window seat. The island kitchen/dining room is spacious enough for a table and includes a handy pantry. A small deck, powder room and laundry area complete the first floor. A vaulted master bedroom resides on the second level, along with a private bath and deck. Bedrooms 2 and 3 are also vaulted and provide ample closet space and access to a full hall bath.

DESIGN HPT150139

First Floor: 762 sq. ft.
Second Floor: 738 sq. ft.
Total: 1,500 sq. ft.
Width: 34'-0"
Depth: 36'-0"

L

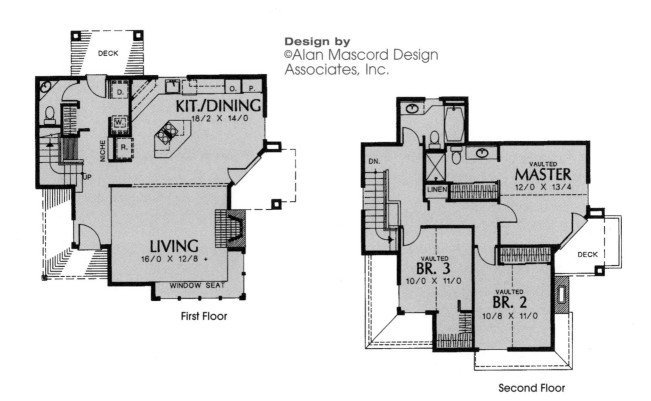

Design by
©Alan Mascord Design
Associates, Inc.

DECK

KIT./DINING
18/2 X 14/0

NICHE

UP

LIVING
16/0 X 12/8 +

WINDOW SEAT

First Floor

DN.

LINEN

VAULTED
MASTER
12/0 X 13/4

DECK

VAULTED
BR. 3
10/0 X 11/0

VAULTED
BR. 2
10/8 X 11/0

Second Floor

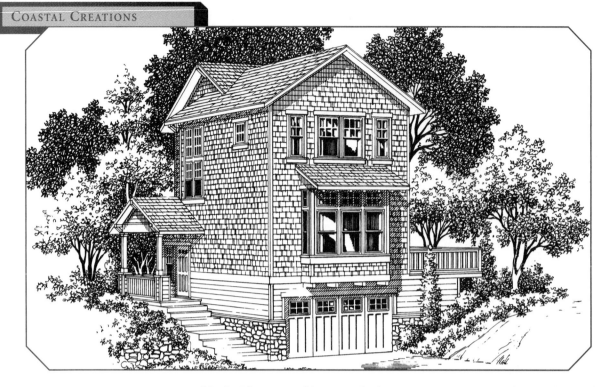

DESIGN HPT150140

Main Level: 898 sq. ft.
Upper Level: 777 sq. ft.
Total: 1,675 sq. ft.
Width: 34'-0"
Depth: 38'-0"

Shingle siding covers this narrow-lot home, creating an exterior that weathers and improves with age. Inside, open planning begins with the living room, dining room and kitchen—separated only by an island countertop, making this area perfect for festive as well as casual gatherings. The upper level houses two family bedrooms and a master bedroom with a private bath. A large workshop at the garage level will be a haven for the handyman in the family.

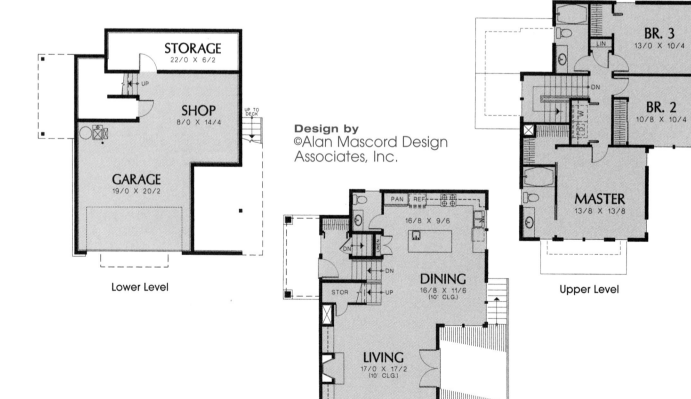

Design by
©Alan Mascord Design
Associates, Inc.

STORAGE
22/0 X 6/2

UP

SHOP
8/0 X 14/4

UP TO
DECK

GARAGE
19/0 X 20/2

Lower Level

PAN | REF
16/8 X 9/6

DN

LINEN

STOR

DN

UP

DINING
16/8 X 11/6
(10' CLG.)

LIVING
17/0 X 17/2
(10' CLG.)

Main Level

BR. 3
13/0 X 10/4

LIN

DN

BR. 2
10/8 X 10/4

MASTER
13/8 X 13/8

Upper Level

Cedar shakes and striking gables with decorative scalloped insets adorn the exterior of this lovely coastal home. The generous great room is expanded by a rear wall of windows, with additional light from transom windows above the front door and a rear clerestory dormer. The kitchen features a pass-through to the great room that doubles as a breakfast/snack bar. The dining room, great room and study all access an inviting back porch. The master bedroom is a treat with a private balcony, His and Hers walk-in closets and an impeccable bath. Upstairs, a room-sized loft with an arched opening overlooks the great room below. Two more bedrooms, one with its own private balcony, share a hall bath.

DESIGN HPT150141

First Floor: 1,650 sq. ft.
Second Floor: 712 sq. ft.
Total: 2,362 sq. ft.
Width: 58'-10"
Depth: 47'-4"

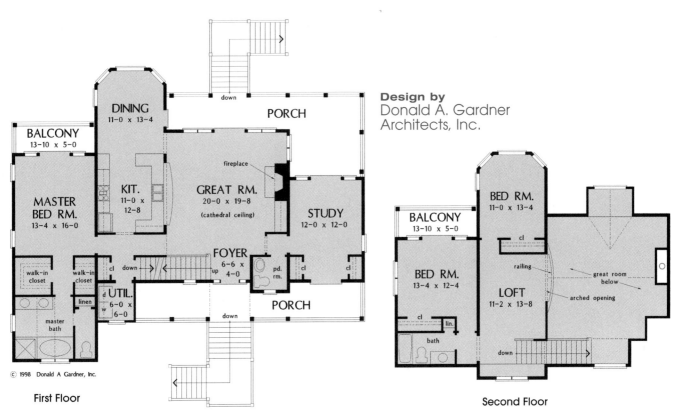

Design by
Donald A. Gardner
Architects, Inc.

First Floor

Second Floor

SHINGLE STYLE

DESIGN HPT150142

First Floor: 630 sq. ft.
Second Floor: 1,039 sq. ft.
Total: 1,669 sq. ft.
Width: 44'-6"
Depth: 32'-0"

This cozy design may look small, but the interior provides all the amenities a homeowner would want. A covered porch leads into a vaulted dining area, directly next to an island kitchen, complete with plenty of counter space and a pantry. The vaulted living room is graced with a fireplace, perfect for chilly evenings. The first-floor vaulted master suite enjoys a linen closet, large walk-in closet, tub and separate shower. Two additional bedrooms share a hall bath upstairs. Bedroom 2 boasts a desk/seat area, perfect for studying.

Design by
©Alan Mascord Design Associates, Inc.

Second Floor

First Floor

GARAGE
22'-8" x 20'-8"

Design by
©Living Concepts
Home Planning

DESIGN HPT150143

First Floor: 871 sq. ft.
Second Floor: 1,047 sq. ft.
Total: 1,918 sq. ft.
Width: 32'-0"
Depth: 47'-0"

First Floor

COVERED PORCH

P.

KITCHEN
11'-6" x 11'-10"

BREAKFAST
11'-6" x 10'-4"

SCREENED PORCH

DINING ROOM
11'-6" x 11'-10"

PDR.

OPT. SHELVES

GATHERING ROOM
19'-8" x 14'-0"

UP

PORCH

First Floor

Second Floor

SUITE 2
11'-6" x 11'-10"

SUITE 3
11'-6" x 13'-0"

BATH

LIN.

STOR.

BALCONY

MASTER BATH

DN

LAUNDRY

MASTER SUITE
16'-2" x 14'-0"

W.I.C.

Second Floor

With its shingle and siding exterior, this home has an air of oceanfront living. A large covered porch accesses a spacious gathering room, complete with a fireplace and optional shelving units. An archway leads from the gathering room to the dining room, which is highlighted with a wall of windows and boasts a doorway to the kitchen. The breakfast area overlooks a screened porch and flows smoothly into a U-shaped kitchen. The sleeping quarters reside upstairs and include two family suites, two full baths, a master suite with a tray ceiling, and a convenient laundry room.

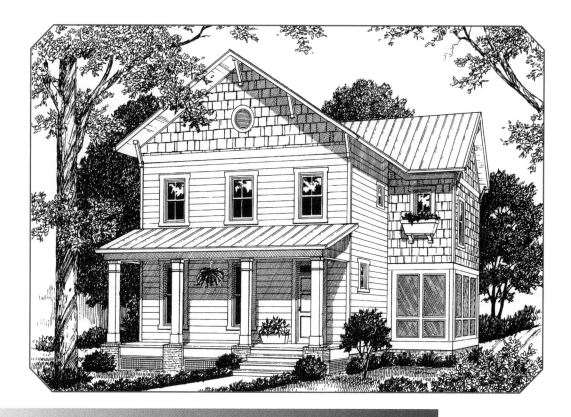

DESIGN HPT150144

Square Footage: 2,019
Bonus Room: 384 sq. ft.
Width: 56'-0"
Depth: 56'-3"

This design takes inspiration from the casual fishing cabins of the Pacific Northwest and interprets it for modern livability. It offers three options for a main entrance. One door opens to a mud porch, where a small hall leads to a galley kitchen and the vaulted great room. Two French doors on the side porch open to a dining room with bay-window seating. Another porch entrance opens directly to the great room. The great room is centered around a massive stone fireplace and is accented with a beautiful wall of windows. The secluded master bedroom features a private bath with a claw-foot tub and twin pedestal sinks, as well as a separate shower and walk-in closet. Two more bedrooms share a spacious bath. Ideal for a lounge or extra sleeping space, an unfinished loft looks over the great room.

Design by
©Stephen Fuller, Inc.

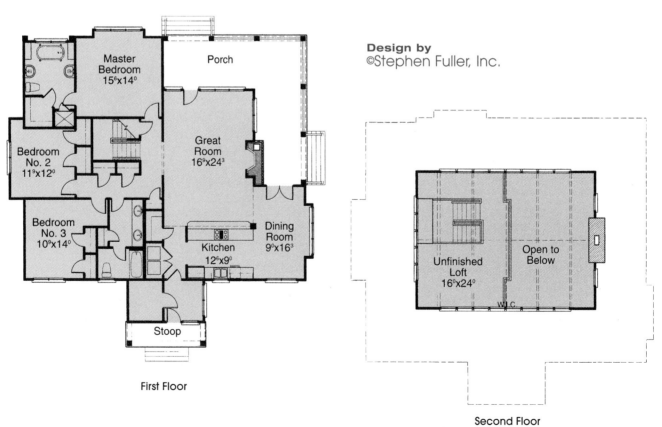

First Floor

Second Floor

I nteresting rooflines, a porte cochere, front and rear covered porches and an angled entry are just the beginning of this bungalow design. The great room welcomes all with its fireplace and windowed views. The efficient kitchen includes access to the formal dining room, breakfast nook and snack bar. An impressive master bedroom has French doors that open to a small entry area that could be used for a study, nursery or sitting room. Two bedrooms on the upper level share a full bath and a study loft.

DESIGN HPT150145

First Floor: 1,836 sq. ft.
Second Floor: 600 sq. ft.
Total: 2,436 sq. ft.
Width: 86'-7"
Depth: 54'-0"

L D

Design by
©Home Planners

QUOTE ONE®

Cost to build? See page 182
to order complete cost estimate
to build this house in your area!

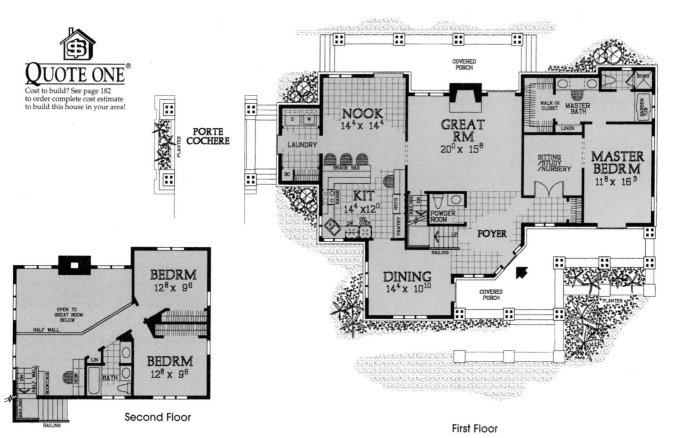

Second Floor

First Floor

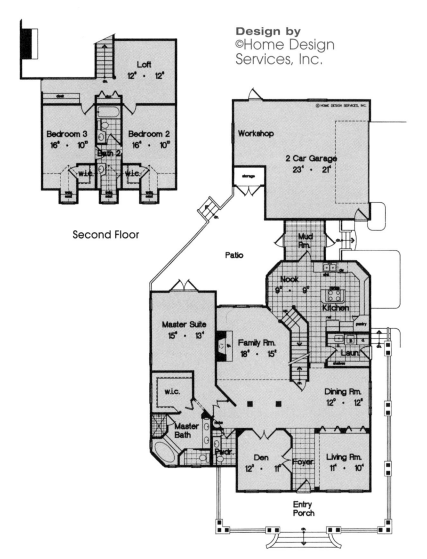

Loft
12⁰ · 12⁰

Bedroom 3
16⁴ · 10⁶

Bedroom 2
16⁴ · 10⁶

Bath 2

w.i.c.   w.i.c.

Second Floor

Design by
©Home Design
Services, Inc.

Workshop

2 Car Garage
23⁴ · 21⁰

storage

Patio

Mud Rm.

Nook
9⁰ · 9⁰

Kitchen

Master Suite
15⁵ · 13⁴

Family Rm.
18⁰ · 15²

Laun.

w.i.c.

pantry

Dining Rm.
12⁰ · 12⁸

Master Bath

Pwdr.

Den
12⁰ · 11⁴

Foyer

Living Rm.
11⁴ · 10⁸

Entry Porch

First Floor

DESIGN HPT150146

First Floor: 1,905 sq. ft.
Second Floor: 758 sq. ft.
Total: 2,663 sq. ft.
Width: 50'-2"
Depth: 85'-10"

Three dormers with fish-scale shingle detailing and a large covered front porch define the character of this design. The foyer is flanked on either side by a den and a living room. Beyond, the dining room sits in close proximity to the kitchen area. The hearth-warmed family room nestles closely to the nook, which features rear property views. The island kitchen boasts a laundry room and is close to the mudroom, which is accessible from the rear patio and a side door just off the two-car garage. The first-floor master suite enjoys a lavish full bath and French doors to the patio. Bedrooms 2 and 3 reside upstairs, each sporting window seats and views through dormer windows. They share a walk-through full bath, each with their own basins. A roomy loft and built-in desk complete this home.

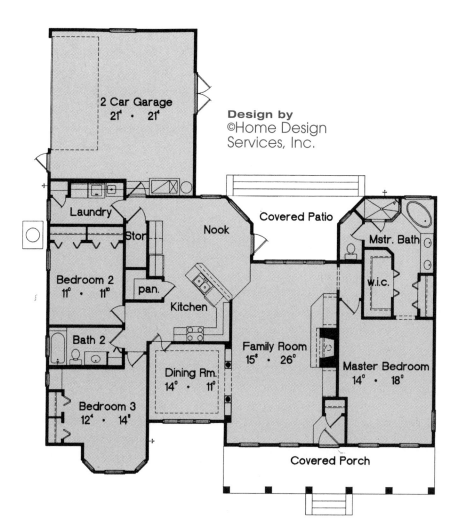

DESIGN HPT150147

Square Footage: 1,963
Width: 58'-0"
Depth: 66'-8"

2 Car Garage 21° · 21°

Design by
©Home Design
Services, Inc.

Laundry

Stor.

Nook

Covered Patio

Mstr. Bath

pan.

Bedroom 2 11° · 11°

Kitchen

w.i.c.

Bath 2

Family Room 15⁸ · 26⁰

Master Bedroom 14⁰ · 18⁰

Dining Rm. 14⁰ · 11⁰

Bedroom 3 12⁴ · 14⁸

Covered Porch

The charm of this home begins with a prominent front-facing pediment, sturdy columns and exposed beams. Venture inside and a family room awaits, complete with a central fireplace and views to the rear property. A dining room with a tray ceiling boasts a columned entrance from the family room and easily accesses the kitchen. The kitchen/nook area provides a pantry, storage space, a laundry room with double sinks and a door to the covered patio. The master bedroom and bath reside on the right side of the plan, complete with a garden tub, separate shower, compartmented toilet and two walk-in closets. The left side is devoted to two family bedrooms that share a full hall bath. Please specify crawlspace or slab foundation when ordering.

SHINGLE STYLE

DESIGN HPT150148

Square Footage: 2,721
Width: 69'-3"
Depth: 79'-3"

I n this design, equally at home in the country or at the coast, classic elements play against a rustic shingle-and-stone exterior. Porch columns provide the elegance, while banks of cottage-style windows let in lots of natural light. The symmetrical layout of the foyer and formal dining room blend easily with the cozy great room. Here, a fireplace creates a welcome atmosphere that invites you to select a novel from one of the built-in bookcases and curl up in your favorite easy chair. The adjacent U-shaped kitchen combines with a sunny breakfast room that opens to a rear porch, making casual meals a pleasure. Split away from family bedrooms for privacy, the master suite occupies the right side of the house and enjoys a dramatic master bath. The left wing contains two secondary bedrooms that share a compartmented bath. This home is designed with a walkout basement foundation.

Porch

Breakfast
16'-3"x11'-0"

Bedroom No. 3
15'-3"x14'-3"

Great Room
21'-0"x18'-0"

Kitchen
16'-3"x12'-9"

Master Bedroom
13'-3"x18'-0"

dn.

Foyer

Dining Room
15'-0"x12'-0"

up

Bedroom No. 2
15'-3"x16'-0"

Porch

Design by
©Stephen Fuller, Inc.

Two Car Garage
22'-3"x24'-9"

S hingles, shutters and vertical siding lend country cottage appeal to this home. The foyer leads to family living space, featuring a great room with a spider-beam ceiling, bumped-out bay window and focal-point fireplace. A guest bedroom enjoys a dressing area and a full bath. Upstairs, an L-shaped hall connects the master bedroom and two family bedrooms that share a full compartmented bath. The master bedroom boasts a walk-in closet, compartmented toilet and twin-basin vanity. This home is designed with a basement foundation.

DESIGN HPT150149

First Floor: 1,578 sq. ft.
Second Floor: 1,324 sq. ft.
Total: 2,902 sq. ft.
Bonus Room: 352 sq. ft.
Width: 76'-0"
Depth: 77'-9"

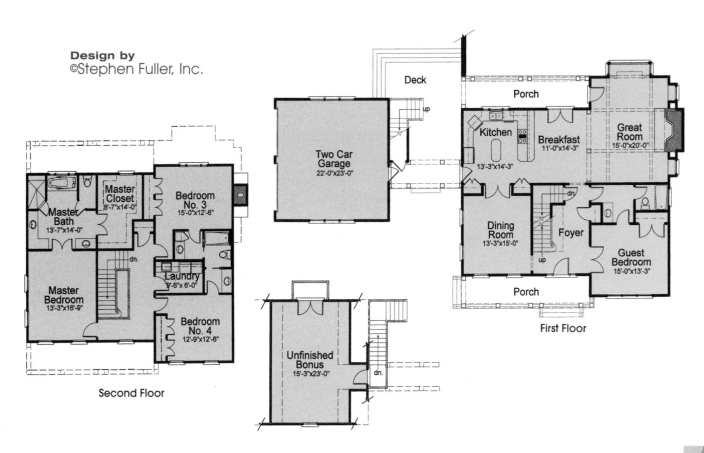

Design by
©Stephen Fuller, Inc.

Deck

Two Car Garage
22'-0"x23'-0"

Porch

Kitchen
13'-3"x14'-3"

Breakfast
11'-0"x14'-3"

Great Room
15'-0"x20'-0"

Dining Room
13'-3"x15'-0"

Foyer

Guest Bedroom
15'-0"x13'-3"

Porch

First Floor

Master Bath
13'-7"x14'-0"

Master Closet
8'-7"x14'-0"

Bedroom No. 3
15'-0"x12'-6"

Laundry
9'-6"x 6'-0"

Master Bedroom
13'-3"x16'-9"

Bedroom No. 4
12'-9"x12'-6"

Second Floor

Unfinished Bonus
15'-3"x23'-0"

SHINGLE STYLE

This Northwest Coastal/country-style home extends livability outside with its front and back porches and elevated deck—perfect for watching sunsets and catching ocean or lakeside breezes. The first floor flows from the open family room and breakfast nook to the kitchen with U-shaped counters. The dining room opens to the kitchen and the foyer. In the front a guest suite contains a private bath. Upstairs, the spacious master bedroom has a walk-in closet and access to the deck. The family bedrooms share a bath with the study. Attached to the main house by a breezeway, the garage includes an unfinished area that can be converted to an apartment above. The full bath is already installed.

DESIGN HPT150150

First Floor: 2,030 sq. ft.
Second Floor: 1,967 sq. ft.
Total: 3,997 sq. ft.
Bonus Room: 688 sq. ft.
Width: 80'-8"
Depth: 111'-8"

Design by
©Living Concepts
Home Planning

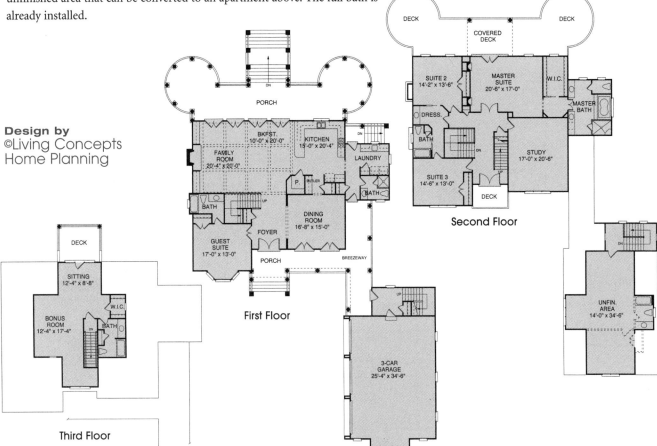

First Floor

Second Floor

Third Floor

The interior of this home boasts high ceilings, a wealth of windows and interestingly shaped rooms. A covered portico leads into a roomy foyer, which is flanked by an office/study, accessible through French doors. Just beyond the foyer a huge vaulted family room highlights columns decorating the entrance and positioned throughout the room. The island kitchen nestles closely to the beautiful dining room, which features rear property views through the bay window and a nearby door to the terrace. The first-floor master suite enjoys two walk-in closets and a lavish bath, as well as access to a covered terrace. The basement level is home to the remaining bedrooms, including Suites 2 and 3, an abundance of storage, a recreation room and a large mechanical/storage room. The recreation room and Suites 2 and 3 directly access the covered terrace at the rear.

DESIGN HPT150151

Main Level: 2,932 sq. ft.
Lower Level: 1,556 sq. ft.
Total: 4,488 sq. ft.
Width: 114'-0"
Depth: 82'-11"

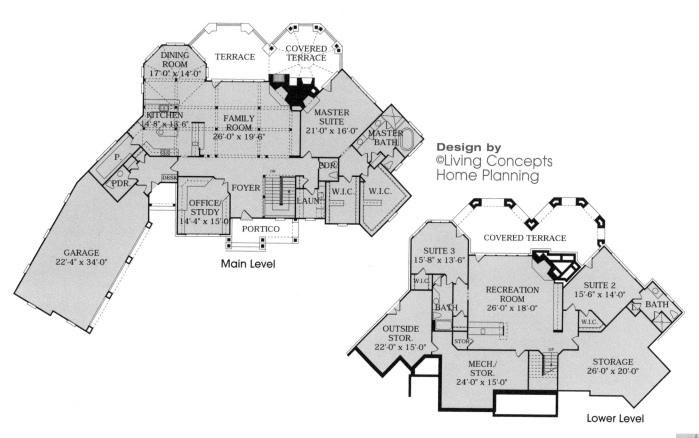

Design by
©Living Concepts
Home Planning

DESIGN HPT150152

First Floor: 906 sq. ft.
Second Floor: 714 sq. ft.
Third Floor: 86 sq. ft.
Total: 1,706 sq. ft.
Width: 40'-0"
Depth: 37'-0"

A unique tower with an observation deck will make this design a standout in any location. Inside, an impressive entry with a wrapping stair leads to three levels of livability. The main level includes a gallery leading to a formal dining room, a counter-filled kitchen on the left and a vaulted great room on the right. Five French doors on the main level access a covered porch spanning the width of the home. The upper level houses the master bedroom, with a sumptuous bath and a private deck, a guest bedroom and a large hall bath. On the lower level, the split two-car garage offers additional storage space.

Design by
©The Sater Design Collection

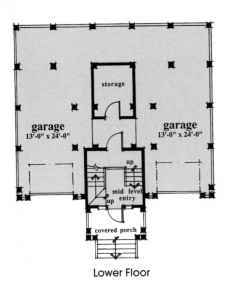

Lower Floor

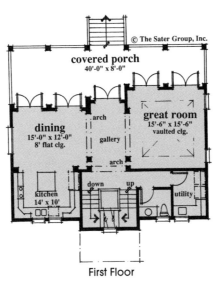

First Floor

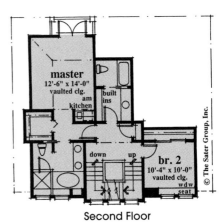

Second Floor

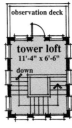

Third Floor

Welcome home to casual, unstuffy living with this comfortable tidewater design. Asymmetrical lines celebrate the turn of the new century, and blend a current Gulf Coast style with vintage panache brought forward from its regional past. The heart of this home is the great room, where a put-your-feet-up atmosphere prevails, and the dusky hues of sunset can mingle with the sounds of ocean breakers. French doors open the master bedroom to a private area off the covered porch, where sunlight and sea breezes mingle with a spirit of *bon vivant*. Please specify basement or crawlspace foundation when ordering.

DESIGN HPT150153

First Floor: 1,290 sq. ft.
Second Floor: 548 sq. ft.
Total: 1,838 sq. ft.
Width: 38'-0"
Depth: 51'-0"

Design by
©The Sater Design
Collection

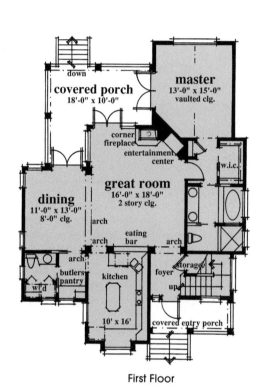

First Floor

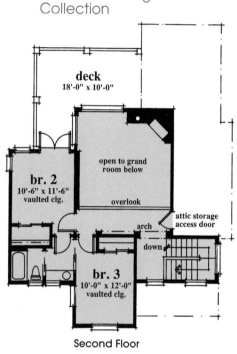

Second Floor

SHINGLE STYLE

DESIGN HPT150154

Square Footage: 2,555
Width: 70'-2"
Depth: 53'-0"

This design enjoys a mixture of shingle and siding, twin dormers and beautiful window detailing. High ceilings adorn most of the rooms in this plan, including the sixteen-foot entry hallway. The great room leads to a balcony and is flanked on the left by a spacious dining room. The island kitchen looks to a bayed breakfast nook, which opens to a rear veranda. The split sleeping quarters place the master suite on the right side and the family bedrooms on the left. The master suite boasts a tray ceiling, His and Hers walk-in closets, garden tub, twin vanities, separate shower, compartmented toilet and a private porch. Bedrooms 2 and 3 are each granted access to separate full baths, as well as close proximity to a utility room. The basement level is devoted primarily to storage space, a large porch and the two-car garage.

Design by
©The Sater Design Collection

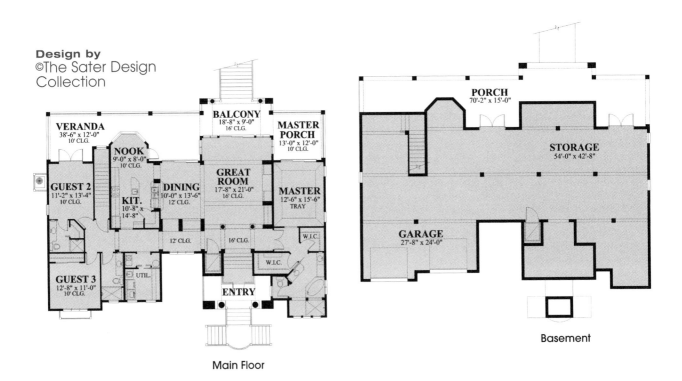

Main Floor

Basement

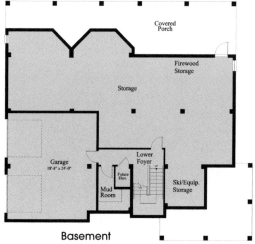

Basement

Design by
©The Sater Design Collection

S iding and shingles give this home a Craftsman look, while columns and gables suggest a more traditional style. The foyer opens to a short flight of stairs that leads to the great room, which features a lovely coffered ceiling, a fireplace, built-ins and French doors to the rear lanai. To the left, the open, island kitchen enjoys a pass-through to the great room and easy service to the dining bay. The secluded master bedroom has two walk-in closets, a luxurious bath and lanai access. Upstairs, two family bedrooms enjoy their own full baths and share a loft area.

DESIGN HPT150155

First Floor: 2,096 sq. ft.
Second Floor: 892 sq. ft.
Total: 2,988 sq. ft.
Bonus Space: 1,295 sq. ft.
Width: 56'-0"
Depth: 54'-0"

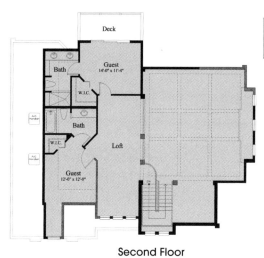

Second Floor

First Floor

WHEN YOU'RE READY TO ORDER...

LET US SHOW YOU OUR HOME BLUEPRINT PACKAGE.

Building a home? Planning a home? Our Blueprint Package has nearly everything you need to get the job done right, whether you're working on your own or with help from an architect, designer, builder or subcontractors. Each Blueprint Package is the result of many hours of work by licensed architects or professional designers.

QUALITY

Hundreds of hours of painstaking effort have gone into the development of your blueprint set. Each home has been quality-checked by professionals to insure accuracy and buildability.

VALUE

Because we sell in volume, you can buy professional quality blueprints at a fraction of their development cost. With our plans, your dream home design costs only a few hundred dollars, not the thousands of dollars that architects charge.

SERVICE

Once you've chosen your favorite home plan, you'll receive fast, efficient service whether you choose to mail or fax your order to us or call us toll free at 1-800-521-6797. For customer service, call toll free 1-888-690-1116.

SATISFACTION

Over 50 years of service to satisfied home plan buyers provide us unparalleled experience and knowledge in producing quality blueprints.

ORDER TOLL FREE
1-800-521-6797

After you've looked over our Blueprint Package and Important Extras on the following pages, simply mail the order form on page 189 or call toll free on our Blueprint Hotline: 1-800-521-6797. We're ready and eager to serve you. For customer service, call toll free 1-888-690-1116.

Each set of blueprints is an interrelated collection of detail sheets which includes components such as floor plans, interior and exterior elevations, dimensions, cross-sections, diagrams and notations. These sheets show exactly how your house is to be built.

AMONG THE SHEETS INCLUDED MAY BE:

FRONTAL SHEET

This artist's sketch of the exterior of the house gives you an idea of how the house will look when built and landscaped. Large floor plans show all levels of the house and provide an overview of your new home's livability, as well as a handy reference for deciding on furniture placement.

FOUNDATION PLANS

This sheet shows the foundation layout including support walls, excavated and unexcavated areas, if any, and foundation notes. If slab construction rather than basement, the plan shows footings and details for a monolithic slab. This page, or another in the set, may include a sample plot plan for locating your house on a building site.

DETAILED FLOOR PLANS

These plans show the layout of each floor of the house. Rooms and interior spaces are carefully dimensioned and keys are given for cross-section details provided later in the plans. The positions of electrical outlets and switches are shown.

HOUSE CROSS-SECTIONS

Large-scale views show sections or cut-aways of the foundation, interior walls, exterior walls, floors, stairways and roof details. Additional cross-sections may show important changes in floor, ceiling or roof heights or the relationship of one level to another. Extremely valuable for construction, these sections show exactly how the various parts of the house fit together.

INTERIOR ELEVATIONS

Many of our drawings show the design and placement of kitchen and bathroom cabinets, laundry areas, fireplaces, bookcases and other built-ins. Little "extras," such as mantelpiece and wainscoting drawings, plus molding sections, provide details that give your home that custom touch.

EXTERIOR ELEVATIONS

These drawings show the front, rear and sides of your house and give necessary notes on exterior materials and finishes. Particular attention is given to cornice detail, brick and stone accents or other finish items that make your home unique.

SAMPLE PACKAGE

FRONTAL SHEET

FOUNDATION PLANS

DETAILED FLOOR PLANS

EXTERIOR ELEVATIONS

INTERIOR ELEVATIONS

HOUSE CROSS-SECTIONS

INTRODUCING EIGHT IMPORTANT PLANNING AND CONSTRUCTION AIDS DEVELOPED BY OUR PROFESSIONALS TO HELP YOU SUCCEED IN YOUR HOME-BUILDING PROJECT

MATERIALS LIST

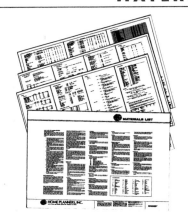

(Note: Because of the diversity of local building codes, our Materials List does not include mechanical materials.)

For many of the designs in our portfolio, we offer a customized materials take-off that is invaluable in planning and estimating the cost of your new home. This Materials List outlines the quantity, type and size of materials needed to build your house (with the exception of mechanical system items). Included are framing lumber, windows and doors, kitchen and bath cabinetry, rough and finish hardware, and much more. This handy list helps you or your builder cost out materials and serves as a reference sheet when you're compiling bids. A Materials List cannot be ordered before blueprints are ordered.

SPECIFICATION OUTLINE

This valuable 16-page document is critical to building your house correctly. Designed to be filled in by you or your builder, this book lists 166 stages or items crucial to the building process. It provides a comprehensive review of the construction process and helps in choosing materials. When combined with the blueprints, a signed contract, and a schedule, it becomes a legal document and record for the building of your home.

QUOTE ONE®

SUMMARY COST REPORT / MATERIALS COST REPORT

A new service for estimating the cost of building select designs, the Quote One® system is available in two separate stages: The Summary Cost Report and the Materials Cost Report.

The **Summary Cost Report** is the first stage in the package and shows the total cost per square foot for your chosen home in your zip-code area and then breaks that cost down into various categories showing the costs for building materials, labor and installation. The report includes three grades: Budget, Standard and Custom. These reports allow you to evaluate your building budget and compare the costs of building a variety of homes in your area.

Make even more informed decisions about your home-building project with the second phase of our package, our **Materials Cost Report.** This tool is invaluable in planning and estimating the cost of your new home. The material and installation (labor and equipment) cost is shown for each of over 1,000 line items provided in the Materials List (Standard grade), which is included when you purchase this estimating tool. It allows you to determine building costs for your specific zip-code area and for your chosen home design. Space is allowed for additional estimates from contractors and subcontractors, such as for mechanical materials, which are not included in our packages. This invaluable tool includes a Materials List. For most plans, a Materials Cost Report cannot be ordered before blueprints are ordered. Call for details. In addition, ask about our Home Planners Estimating Package.

The Quote One® program is continually updated with new plans. If you are interested in a plan that is not indicated as Quote One®, please call and ask our sales reps. They will be happy to verify the status for you. To order these invaluable reports, use the order form on page 189 or call 1-800-521-6797 for availability.

CONSTRUCTION INFORMATION

If you want to know more about techniques—and deal more confidently with subcontractors—we offer these useful sheets. Each set is an excellent tool that will add to your understanding of these technical subjects. These helpful details provide general construction information and are not specific to any single plan.

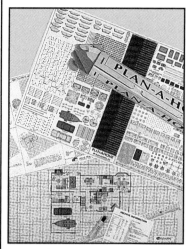

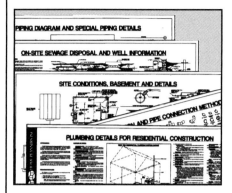

PLUMBING

The Blueprint Package includes locations for all the plumbing fixtures, including sinks, lavatories, tubs, showers, toilets, laundry trays and water heaters. However, if you want to know more about the complete plumbing system, these Plumbing Details will prove very useful. Prepared to meet requirements of the National Plumbing Code, these fact-filled sheets give general information on pipe schedules, fittings, sump-pump details, water-softener hookups, septic system details and much more. Sheets also include a glossary of terms.

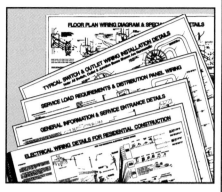

ELECTRICAL

The locations for every electrical switch, plug and outlet are shown in your Blueprint Package. However, these Electrical Details go further to take the mystery out of household electrical systems. Prepared to meet requirements of the National Electrical Code, these comprehensive drawings come packed with helpful information, including wire sizing, switch-installation schematics, cable-routing details, appliance wattage, doorbell hookups, typical service panel circuitry and much more. A glossary of terms is also included.

PLAN-A-HOME® is an easy-to-use tool that helps you design a new home, arrange furniture in a new or existing home, or plan a remodeling project. Each package contains:

✓ **MORE THAN 700 REUSABLE PEEL-OFF PLANNING SYMBOLS** on a self-stick vinyl sheet, including walls, windows, doors, all types of furniture, kitchen components, bath fixtures and many more.

✓ **A REUSABLE, TRANSPARENT, ¼" SCALE PLANNING GRID** that matches the scale of actual working drawings (¼" equals one foot). This grid provides the basis for house layouts of up to 140'x92'.

✓ **TRACING PAPER** and a protective sheet for copying or transferring your completed plan.

✓ **A FELT-TIP PEN**, with water-soluble ink that wipes away quickly.

Plan-A-Home® lets you lay out areas as large as a 7,500 square foot, six-bedroom, seven-bath house.

CONSTRUCTION

The Blueprint Package contains everything an experienced builder needs to construct a particular house. However, it doesn't show all the ways that houses can be built, nor does it explain alternate construction methods. To help you understand how your house will be built—and offer additional techniques—this set of Construction Details depicts the materials and methods used to build foundations, fireplaces, walls, floors and roofs. Where appropriate, the drawings show acceptable alternatives.

MECHANICAL

These Mechanical Details contain fundamental principles and useful data that will help you make informed decisions and communicate with subcontractors about heating and cooling systems. Drawings contain instructions and samples that allow you to make simple load calculations, and preliminary sizing and costing analysis. Covered are today's most commonly used systems from heat pumps to solar fuel systems. The package is filled with illustrations and diagrams to help you visualize components and how they relate to one another.

To Order, Call Toll Free 1-800-521-6797

To add these important extras to your Blueprint Package, simply indicate your choices on the order form on page 189. Or call us toll free 1-800-521-6797 and we'll tell you more about these exciting products. For customer service, call toll free 1-888-690-1116.

THE FINISHING TOUCHES...

THE DECK BLUEPRINT PACKAGE

Many of the homes in this book can be enhanced with a professionally designed Home Planners Deck Plan. Those home plans highlighted with a **D** have a matching Deck Plan, sold separately, which includes a Deck Plan Frontal Sheet, Deck Framing and Floor Plans, Deck Elevations and a Deck Materials List. A Standard Deck Details Package, also available, provides all the how-to information necessary for building *any* deck. Our Complete Deck Building Package contains one set of Custom Deck Plans of your choice, plus one set of Standard Deck Building Details, all for one low price. Our plans and details are carefully prepared in an easy-to-understand format that will guide you through every stage of your deck-building project. This page contains a sampling of six different Deck layouts (and a front-yard landscape) to match your favorite house. See page 186 for prices and ordering information.

EUROPEAN-FLAIR HOME
Landscape OLA088

WEEKEND-ENTERTAINER DECK
Deck ODA013

CENTER-VIEW DECK
Deck ODA015

KITCHEN-EXTENDER DECK
Deck ODA016

SPLIT-LEVEL ACTIVITY DECK
Deck ODA018

TRI-LEVEL DECK WITH GRILL
Deck ODA020

CONTEMPORARY LEISURE DECK
Deck ODA021

THE LANDSCAPE BLUEPRINT PACKAGE

For the homes marked with an **L** in this book, Home Planners has created a front-yard Landscape Plan that matches or is complementary in design to the house plan. These comprehensive blueprint packages include a Frontal Sheet, Plan View, Regionalized Plant & Materials List, a sheet on Planting and Maintaining Your Landscape, Zone Maps and Plant Size and Description Guide. These plans will help you achieve professional results, adding value and enjoyment to your property for years to come. Each set of blueprints is a full 18" x 24" in size with clear, complete instructions and easy-to-read type. Six of the forty front-yard Landscape Plans to match your favorite house are shown below.

Regional Order Map

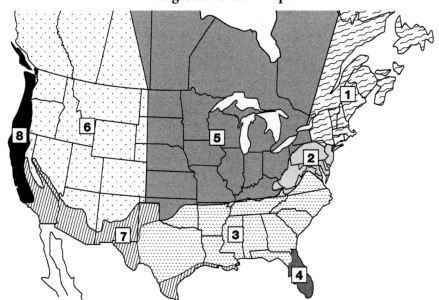

Most of the Landscape Plans shown on these pages are available with a Plant & Materials List adapted by horticultural experts to 8 different regions of the country. Please specify the Geographic Region when ordering your plan. See pages 186-187 for prices, ordering information and regional availability.

Region	1	Northeast
Region	2	Mid-Atlantic
Region	3	Deep South
Region	4	Florida & Gulf Coast
Region	5	Midwest
Region	6	Rocky Mountains
Region	7	Southern California & Desert Southwest
Region	8	Northern California & Pacific Northwest

CAPE COD COTTAGE
Landscape OLA003

GAMBREL-ROOF COLONIAL
Landscape OLA004

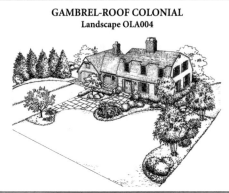

CENTER-HALL COLONIAL
Landscape OLA005

CLASSIC NEW ENGLAND COLONIAL
Landscape OLA006

COUNTRY-STYLE FARMHOUSE
Landscape OLA008

TRADITIONAL SPLIT-LEVEL
Landscape OLA029

HOUSE BLUEPRINT PRICE SCHEDULE

Prices guaranteed through December 31, 2001

TIERS	1-SET STUDY PACKAGE	4-SET BUILDING PACKAGE	8-SET BUILDING PACKAGE	1-SET REPRODUCIBLE	HOME CUSTOMIZER® PACKAGE
P1	$20	$50	$90	$140	N/A
P2	$40	$70	$110	$160	N/A
P3	$60	$90	$130	$180	N/A
P4	$80	$110	$150	$200	N/A
P5	$100	$130	$170	$230	N/A
P6	$120	$150	$190	$250	N/A
A1	$420	$460	$520	$625	$680
A2	$460	$500	$560	$685	$740
A3	$500	$540	$600	$745	$800
A4	$540	$580	$640	$805	$860
C1	$585	$625	$685	$870	$925
C2	$625	$665	$725	$930	$985
C3	$675	$715	$775	$980	$1035
C4	$725	$765	$825	$1030	$1085
L1	$785	$825	$885	$1090	$1145
L2	$835	$875	$935	$1140	$1195
L3	$935	$975	$1035	$1240	$1295
L4	$1035	$1075	$1135	$1340	$1395

OPTIONS FOR PLANS IN TIERS A1–L4

Additional Identical Blueprints in same order for "A1–L4" price plans ....$50 per set

Reverse Blueprints (mirror image) with 4- or 8-set order for "A1–L4" price plans ....$50 fee per order

Specification Outlines ....$10 each

Materials Lists for "A1–C3" price plans ....$60 each

Materials Lists for "C4–L4" price plans ....$70 each

OPTIONS FOR PLANS IN TIERS P1–P6

Additional Identical Blueprints in same order for "P1–P6" price plans ....$10 per set

Reverse Blueprints (mirror image) for "P1–P6" price plans ....$10 per set

1 Set of Deck Construction Details ....$14.95 each

Deck Construction Package ....add $10 to Building Package price
(includes 1 set of "P1–P6" price plans, plus
1 set Standard Deck Construction Details)

1 Set of Gazebo Construction Details ....$14.95 each

Gazebo Construction Package ....add $10 to Building Package price
(includes 1 set of "P1–P6" price plans, plus
1 set Standard Gazebo Construction Details)

IMPORTANT NOTES

The 1-set study package is marked "not for construction."
Prices for 4- or 8-set Building Packages honored only at time of original order. Some basement foundations carry a $225 surcharge. Right-reading reverse blueprints, if available, will incur a $165 surcharge.

INDEX

To use the Index below, refer to the design number listed in numerical order (a helpful page reference is also given). Note the price index letter and refer to the House Blueprint Price Schedule above for the cost of one, four or eight sets of blueprints or the cost of a reproducible drawing. Additional prices are shown for identical and reverse blueprint sets, as well as a very useful Materials List for some of the plans. Also note in the Index below those plans that have matching or complementary Deck Plans or Landscape Plans. Refer to the schedules above for prices of these plans. All plans in this publication are customizable. However, only Home Planners

plans can be customized with the Home Planners Home Customizer® Package. These plans are indicated below with the letter "Y." See page 189 for more information. The letter "Y" also identifies plans that are part of our Quote One® estimating service and those that offer Materials Lists. See page 182 for more information.

To Order: Fill in and send the order form on page 189—or call toll free 1-800-521-6797 or 520-297-8200. FAX: 1-800-224-6699 or 520-544-3086

DESIGN	PRICE	PAGE	MATERIALS LIST	CUSTOMIZABLE®	QUOTE ONE®	DECK	DECK PRICE	LANDSCAPE	LANDSCAPE PRICE	REGIONS
HPT150001	C3	17	Y		Y					
HPT150002	C1	13			Y					
HPT150003	C3	20								
HPT150004	C3	23								
HPT150005	A1	24								
HPT150006	A4	25	Y	Y	Y					
HPT150007	C2	26								
HPT150008	A3	27	Y		Y					
HPT150009	C3	28								
HPT150010	A4	29	Y							
HPT150011	C4	30								
HPT150012	C3	31								
HPT150013	C1	32	Y	Y	Y			OLA010	P3	1234568
HPT150014	C4	34								
HPT150015	C3	35								
HPT150016	C1	36	Y	Y						
HPT150017	C1	37	Y	Y						
HPT150018	C2	38	Y	Y						
HPT150019	C3	39	Y	Y	Y					

DESIGN	PRICE	PAGE	MATERIALS LIST	CUSTOMIZABLE®	QUOTE ONE®	DECK	DECK PRICE	LANDSCAPE	LANDSCAPE PRICE	REGIONS
HPT150020	A4	40	Y							
HPT150021	A3	41	Y							
HPT150022	A3	42	Y							
HPT150023	A4	43	Y							
HPT150024	C1	44		Y						
HPT150025	A4	45		Y						
HPT150026	C3	46								
HPT150027	A3	47								
HPT150028	L1	48								
HPT150029	C4	49								
HPT150030	C3	50								
HPT150031	C1	51								
HPT150032	C4	52								
HPT150033	C4	54	Y	Y	Y			OLA001	P3	123568
HPT150034	C2	55	Y	Y	Y			OLA001	P3	123568
HPT150035	C1	56	Y							
HPT150036	A3	57								
HPT150037	A4	58								
HPT150038	A4	59	Y		Y			OLA001	P3	123568

DESIGN	PRICE	PAGE	MATERIALS LIST	CUSTOMIZABLE	QUOTE ONE	DECK	DECK PRICE	LANDSCAPE	LANDSCAPE PRICE	REGIONS
HPT150039	C2	60	Y	Y	Y			OLA003	P3	123568
HPT150040	C2	61	Y	Y	Y					
HPT150041	A3	62	Y							
HPT150042	A3	63								
HPT150043	A3	64								
HPT150044	A3	65								
HPT150045	A3	66								
HPT150046	A4	67	Y							
HPT150047	A3	68	Y							
HPT150048	C3	69	Y							
HPT150049	A3	70	Y							
HPT150050	A4	71								
HPT150051	A4	72	Y							
HPT150052	A4	73	Y							
HPT150053	A3	74								
HPT150054	A3	75								
HPT150055	A4	76								
HPT150056	C1	77								
HPT150057	C1	78	Y					OLA004	P3	123568
HPT150058	A4	79	Y							
HPT150059	C3	80								
HPT150060	C4	81								
HPT150061	A4	82	Y							
HPT150062	A4	83	Y							
HPT150063	A4	84	Y							
HPT150064	A2	86	Y							
HPT150065	A2	87	Y							
HPT150066	A3	88	Y							
HPT150067	C1	89			Y					
HPT150068	C3	90								
HPT150069	C3	91	Y		Y					
HPT150070	C1	92								
HPT150071	C3	93								
HPT150072	L1	94								
HPT150073	C1	95								
HPT150074	C4	97								
HPT150075	C2	96	Y		Y					
HPT150076	A4	98								
HPT150077	C4	99			Y					
HPT150078	C3	100								
HPT150079	C3	101								
HPT150080	A4	102								
HPT150081	C1	103	Y							
HPT150082	C4	104								
HPT150083	C4	105								
HPT150084	C2	106								
HPT150085	C4	107								
HPT150086	L2	108								
HPT150087	C4	109								
HPT150088	L2	110								
HPT150089	C3	111			Y					
HPT150090	C4	112								
HPT150091	C3	113								
HPT150092	C3	114								
HPT150093	C4	115								
HPT150094	C4	116			Y					
HPT150095	A4	118	Y							
HPT150096	A4	119	Y							
HPT150097	A3	120								
HPT150098	A4	121	Y		Y					
HPT150099	A4	122			Y					
HPT150100	C1	123			Y					
HPT150101	A4	124			Y					
HPT150102	A4	125			Y					
HPT150103	C2	126			Y					
HPT150104	C2	127			Y					
HPT150105	C1	128			Y					
HPT150106	C2	129			Y					
HPT150107	C3	130	Y					OLA005	P3	123568
HPT150108	L1	131								
HPT150109	A4	132								
HPT150110	A4	133								
HPT150111	A3	134								
HPT150112	C2	135			Y					
HPT150113	C1	136								
HPT150114	A4	137								
HPT150115	A4	138	Y							
HPT150116	A4	139								
HPT150117	A4	140								
HPT150118	C4	141								
HPT150119	C1	142								
HPT150120	C1	143								
HPT150121	C1	144	Y		Y					
HPT150122	C3	145			Y					
HPT150123	C3	146								
HPT150124	C4	147								
HPT150125	C3	148	Y	Y	Y	ODA016	P2	OLA008	P4	1234568
HPT150126	A3	149	Y							
HPT150127	A4	150	Y							
HPT150128	C3	151			Y					
HPT150129	C2	152			Y					
HPT150130	C1	153			Y					
HPT150131	C1	154								
HPT150132	A3	156	Y	Y	Y	ODA003	P2	OLA003	P3	123568
HPT150133	A1	157	Y	Y						
HPT150134	A3	158	Y	Y						
HPT150135	C1	159	Y	Y						
HPT150136	A3	160								
HPT150137	C2	161								
HPT150138	C1	162								
HPT150139	A3	163	Y					OLA024	P4	123568
HPT150140	A3	164								
HPT150141	A4	165	Y							
HPT150142	A3	166	Y	Y						
HPT150143	C1	167								
HPT150144	C2	168								
HPT150145	C2	169	Y	Y	Y	ODA012	P3	OLA084	P3	12345678
HPT150146	C1	170			Y					
HPT150147	A4	171			Y					
HPT150148	C1	172								
HPT150149	C3	173								
HPT150150	L2	174								
HPT150151	L2	175								
HPT150152	A4	176	Y							
HPT150153	A4	177								
HPT150154	C1	178								
HPT150155	C3	179			Y					

BEFORE YOU ORDER...

BEFORE FILLING OUT THE COUPON AT RIGHT OR CALLING US ON OUR TOLL-FREE BLUEPRINT HOTLINE, YOU MAY WANT TO LEARN MORE ABOUT OUR SERVICES AND PRODUCTS. HERE'S SOME INFORMATION YOU WILL FIND HELPFUL.

OUR EXCHANGE POLICY

Since blueprints are printed in response to your order, we cannot honor requests for refunds. However, we will exchange your entire first order for an equal or greater number of blueprints within our plan collection within 90 days of the original order. The entire content of your original order must be returned to our offices before an exchange will be processed. If the returned blueprints look used, redlined or copied, we will not honor your exchange. Fees for exchanging your blueprints are as follows: 20% of the amount of the original order...*plus* the difference in cost if exchanging for a design in a higher price bracket or *less* the difference in cost if exchanging for a design in lower price bracket. (**Reproducible blueprints are not exchangeable.**) Please add $25 for postage and handling via Regular Service; $35 via Priority Service; $45 via Express Service. Shipping and handling charges are not refundable.

ABOUT REVERSE BLUEPRINTS

If you want to build in reverse of the plan as shown, we will include any number of reverse blueprints (mirror image) from a 4- or 8-set package for an additional fee of $50. Although lettering and dimensions will appear backward, reverses will be a useful aid if you decide to flop the plan.

REVISING, MODIFYING AND CUSTOMIZING PLANS

The wide variety of designs available in this publication allows you to select ideas and concepts for a home to fit your building site and match your family's needs, wants and budget. Like many homeowners who buy these plans, you and your builder, architect or engineer may want to make changes to them. Some changes may be made by your builder, but we recommend that most changes be made by a licensed architect or engineer. If you need to make alterations to a design that is customizable, you need only order our Home Customizer® Package to get you started. As set forth below, we cannot assume any responsibility for blueprints which have been changed, whether by you, your builder or by professionals selected by you or referred to you by us, because such individuals are outside our supervision and control.

ARCHITECTURAL AND ENGINEERING SEALS

Some cities and states are now requiring that a licensed architect or engineer review and "seal" a blueprint, or officially approve it, prior to construction due to concerns over energy costs, safety and other factors. Prior to application for a building permit or the start of actual construction, we strongly advise that you consult your local building official who can tell you if such a review is required.

ABOUT THE DESIGNS

The architects and designers whose work appears in this publication are among America's leading residential designers. Each plan was designed to meet the requirements of a nationally recognized model building code in effect at the time and place the plan was drawn. Because national building codes change from time to time, plans may not comply with any such code at the time they are sold to a customer. In addition, building officials may not accept these plans as final construction documents of record as the plans may need to be modified and additional drawings and details added to suit local conditions and requirements. We strongly advise that purchasers consult a licensed architect or engineer, and their local building official, before starting any construction related to these plans.

LOCAL BUILDING CODES AND ZONING REQUIREMENTS

At the time of creation, our plans are drawn to specifications published by the Building Officials and Code Administrators (BOCA) International, Inc.; the Southern Building Code Congress (SBCCI) International, Inc.; the International Conference of Building Officials (ICBO); or the Council of American Building Officials (CABO). Our plans are designed to meet or exceed na-

tional building standards. Because of the great differences in geography and climate throughout the United States and Canada, each state, county and municipality has its own building codes, zone requirements, ordinances and building regulations. Your plan may need to be modified to comply with local requirements regarding snow loads, energy codes, soil and seismic conditions and a wide range of other matters. In addition, you may need to obtain permits or inspections from local governments before and in the course of construction. Prior to using blueprints ordered from us, we strongly advise that you consult a licensed architect or engineer—and speak with your local building official—before applying for any permit or beginning construction. We authorize the use of our blueprints on the express condition that you strictly comply with all local building codes, zoning requirements and other applicable laws, regulations, ordinances and requirements. **Notice: Plans for homes to be built in Nevada must be re-drawn by a Nevada-registered professional. Consult your building official for more information on this subject.**

FOUNDATION AND EXTERIOR WALL CHANGES

Depending on your specific climate or regional building practices, you may wish to change a full basement to a slab or crawlspace foundation. Most professional contractors and builders can easily adapt your plans to alternate foundation types. Likewise, most can easily change 2x4 wall construction to 2x6, or vice versa.

DISCLAIMER

We and the designers we work with have put substantial care and effort into the creation of our blueprints. However, because we cannot provide on-site consultation, supervision and control over actual construction, and because of the great variance in local building requirements, building practices and soil, seismic, weather and other conditions, WE CANNOT MAKE ANY WARRANTY, EXPRESS OR IMPLIED, WITH RESPECT TO THE CONTENT OR USE OF OUR BLUEPRINTS, INCLUDING BUT NOT LIMITED TO ANY WARRANTY OF MERCHANTABILITY OR OF FITNESS FOR A PARTICULAR PURPOSE. **ITEMS, PRICES, TERMS AND CONDITIONS ARE SUBJECT TO CHANGE WITHOUT NOTICE. PLAN ORDER MAY REQUIRE A CUSTOMER'S SIGNED RELEASE BEFORE SHIPPING ORDER.**

TERMS AND CONDITIONS

These designs are protected under the terms of United States Copyright Law and may not be copied or reproduced in any way, by any means, unless you have purchased Sepias or Reproducibles which clearly indicate your right to copy or reproduce. We authorize the use of your chosen design as an aid in the construction of one single family home only. You may not use this design to build a second or multiple dwellings without purchasing another blueprint or blueprints or paying additional design fees.

HOW MANY BLUEPRINTS DO YOU NEED?

A single set of blueprints is sufficient to study a home in greater detail. However, if you are planning to obtain cost estimates from a contractor or subcontractors—or if you are planning to build immediately—you will need more sets. Because additional sets are cheaper when ordered in quantity with the original order, make sure you order enough blueprints to satisfy all requirements. The following checklist will help you determine how many you need:

__ Owner

__ Builder (generally requires at least three sets; one as a legal document, one to use during inspections, and at least one to give to subcontractors)

__ Local Building Department (often requires two sets)

__ Mortgage Lender (usually one set for a conventional loan; three sets for FHA or VA loans)

__ TOTAL NUMBER OF SETS

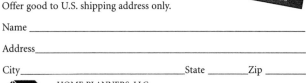

☎ **TOLL FREE 1-800-521-6797**

REGULAR OFFICE HOURS:
8:00 a.m.-12:00 a.m. EST, Monday-Friday, 10:00 a.m.-7:00 p.m. EST Sat & Sun.

If we receive your order by 3:00 p.m. EST, Monday-Friday, we'll process it and ship within **two business days**. When ordering by phone, please have your credit card ready. We'll also ask you for the Order Form Key Number at the bottom of the coupon.

By FAX: Copy the Order Form on the next page and send it on our FAX line:
1-800-224-6699 or 520-544-3086.

Canadian Customers — Order Toll Free 1-877-223-6389

For faster service, Canadian customers may now call in orders directly to our Canadian supplier of plans and charge the purchase to a credit card. Or, you may complete the order form at right, adding the current exchange rate to all prices and mail in Canadian funds to:

Home Planners Canada, c/o Select Home Designs
301-611 Alexander Street • Vancouver, BC, Canada • V6A 1E1

OR: Copy the Order Form and send it via our FAX line: 1-800-224-6699.

 **The Home Customizer®**

"This house is perfect...if only the family room were two feet wider." Sound familiar? In response to the numerous requests for this type of modification, Home Planners has developed **The Home Customizer® Package**. This exclusive package offers our top-of-the-line materials to make it easy for anyone, anywhere to customize any Home Planners design to fit their needs. Check the index on page 186-187 for those plans which are customizable.

Some of the changes you can make to any of our plans include:

- exterior elevation changes
- kitchen and bath modifications
- roof, wall and foundation changes
- room additions and more!

The Home Customizer® Package includes everything you'll need to make the necessary changes to your favorite Home Planners design. The package includes:

- instruction book with examples
- architectural scale and clear work film
- erasable red marker and removable correction tape
- ¼"-scale furniture cutouts
- 1 set reproducible drawings
- 1 set study blueprints for communicating changes to your design professional
- a copyright release letter so you can make copies as you need them
- referral letter with the name, address and telephone number of the professional in your region who is trained in modifying Home Planners designs efficiently and inexpensively.

The Home Customizer® Package will not only save you 25% to 75% of the cost of drawing the plans from scratch with an architect or engineer, it will also give you the flexibility to have your changes and modifications made by our referral network or by the professional of your choice. Now it's even easier and more affordable to have the custom home you've always wanted.

 **ORDER TOLL FREE!** FOR INFORMATION ABOUT ANY OF OUR SERVICES OR TO ORDER CALL

1-800-521-6797 OR 520-297-8200
Browse our website:
www.eplans.com

BLUEPRINTS ARE NOT REFUNDABLE EXCHANGES ONLY

FOR CUSTOMER SERVICE, CALL TOLL FREE 1-888-690-1116.

HOME PLANNERS, LLC wholly owned by Hanley-Wood, LLC
3275 WEST INA ROAD, SUITE 110 • TUCSON, ARIZONA • 85741

THE BASIC BLUEPRINT PACKAGE
Rush me the following (please refer to the Plans Index and Price Schedule in this section):
___ Set(s) of blueprints for plan number(s) _____. $_____
___ Set(s) of reproducibles for plan number(s) _____. $_____
___ Home Customizer® Package for plan(s)_____. $_____
___ Additional identical blueprints (standard or reverse) in same order @ $50 per set. $_____
___ Reverse blueprints @ $50 fee per order. Right-reading reverse @ $165 surcharge $_____

IMPORTANT EXTRAS
Rush me the following:
___ Materials List: $60 (Must be purchased with Blueprint set.) Add $10 for Schedule C4–L4 plans. $_____
___ **Quote One®** Summary Cost Report @ $29.95 for one, $14.95 for each additional,
for plans _____ $_____
Building location: City _____ Zip Code _____
___ **Quote One®** Materials Cost Report @ $120 Schedules P1–C3; $130 Schedules C4–L4,
for plan_____(Must be purchased with Blueprints set.) $_____
Building location: City _____ Zip Code _____
___ Specification Outlines @ $10 each. $_____
___ Detail Sets @ $14.95 each; any two $22.95; any three $29.95; all four for $39.95 (save $19.85). $_____
___ ❑ Plumbing ❑ Electrical ❑ Construction ❑ Mechanical
___ Plan-A-Home® @ $29.95 each. $_____

DECK BLUEPRINTS
(Please refer to the Plans Index and Price Schedule in this section)
___ Set(s) of Deck Plan _____. $_____
___ Additional identical blueprints in same order @ $10 per set. $_____
___ Reverse blueprints @ $10 per set. $_____
___ Set of Standard Deck Details @ $14.95 per set. $_____
___ Set of Complete Deck Construction Package (Best Buy!) Add $10 to Building Package
Includes Custom Deck Plan _____ Plus Standard Deck Details

LANDSCAPE BLUEPRINTS
(Please refer to the Plans Index and Price Schedule in this section)
___ Set(s) of Landscape Plan _____. $_____
___ Additional identical blueprints in same order @ $10 per set. $_____
___ Reverse blueprints @ $10 per set. $_____
Please indicate the appropriate region of the country for Plant & Material List.
(See map on page 185): Region _____

POSTAGE AND HANDLING	1–3 sets	4+ sets
Signature is required for all deliveries. **DELIVERY** No CODs (Requires street address—No P.O. Boxes)		
•Regular Service (Allow 7–10 business days delivery)	❑ $20.00	❑ $25.00
•Priority (Allow 4–5 business days delivery)	❑ $25.00	❑ $35.00
•Express (Allow 3 business days delivery)	❑ $35.00	❑ $45.00
OVERSEAS DELIVERY	fax, phone or mail for quote	

Note: All delivery times are from date Blueprint Package is shipped.

POSTAGE (From box above) $_____
SUBTOTAL $_____
SALES TAX (AZ & MI residents, please add appropriate state and local sales tax.) $_____
TOTAL (Subtotal and tax) $_____

YOUR ADDRESS (please print)

Name _____

Street_____

City _____State_____Zip _____

Daytime telephone number (_____) _____

FOR CREDIT CARD ORDERS ONLY

Credit card number _____ Exp. Date: (M/Y) _____
Check one ❑ Visa ❑ MasterCard ❑ Discover Card ❑ American Express

Signature_____

Order Form Key
Please check appropriate box: ❑ Licensed Builder-Contractor ❑ Homeowner | HPT15 |

 **ORDER TOLL FREE!**
1-800-521-6797 or 520-297-8200
BY FAX: Copy the order form above and send it on our FAXLINE: 1-800-224-6699 or 1-520-544-3086

HOME PLANNERS WANTS YOUR BUILDING EXPERIENCE TO BE AS PLEASANT AND TROUBLE-FREE AS POSSIBLE.

That's why we've expanded our library of Do-It-Yourself titles to help you along. In addition to our beautiful plans books, we've added books to guide you through specific projects as well as the construction process. In fact, these are titles that will be as useful after your dream home is built as they are right now.

BIGGEST & BEST

1001 of our best-selling plans in one volume. 1,074 to 7,275 square feet. 704 pgs $12.95 1K1

ONE-STORY

450 designs for all lifestyles. 800 to 4,900 square feet. 384 pgs $9.95 OS

MORE ONE-STORY

475 superb one-level plans from 800 to 5,000 square feet. 448 pgs $9.95 MOS

TWO-STORY

443 designs for one-and-a-half and two stories. 1,500 to 6,000 square feet. 448 pgs $9.95 TS

VACATION

465 designs for recreation, retirement and leisure. 448 pgs $9.95 VSH

HILLSIDE

208 designs for split-levels, bi-levels, multi-levels and walkouts. 224 pgs $9.95 HH

FARMHOUSE

200 country designs from classic to contemporary by 7 winning designers. 224 pgs $8.95 FH

COUNTRY HOUSES

208 unique home plans that combine traditional style and modern livability. 224 pgs $9.95 CN

BUDGET-SMART

200 efficient plans from 7 top designers, that you can really afford to build! 224 pgs $8.95 BS

BARRIER FREE

Over 1,700 products and 51 plans for accessible living. 128 pgs $15.95 UH

ENCYCLOPEDIA

500 exceptional plans for all styles and budgets—the best book of its kind! 528 pgs $9.95 ENC

ENCYCLOPEDIA II

500 completely new plans. Spacious and stylish designs for every budget and taste. 352 pgs $9.95 E2

AFFORDABLE

Completely revised and updated, featuring 300 designs for modest budgets. 256 pgs $9.95 AF

VICTORIAN

NEW! 210 striking Victorian and Farmhouse designs from today's top designers. 224 pgs $15.95 VDH2

ESTATE

Dream big! Twenty-one designers showcase their biggest and best plans. 208 pgs $15.95 EDH

LUXURY

154 fine luxury plans—loaded with luscious amenities! 192 pgs $14.95 LD2

EUROPEAN STYLES

200 homes with a unique flair of the Old World. 224 pgs $15.95 EURO

COUNTRY CLASSICS

Donald Gardner's 101 best Country and Traditional home plans. 192 pgs $17.95 DAG

WILLIAM POOLE

70 romantic house plans that capture the classic tradition of home design. 160 pgs $17.95 WEP

TRADITIONAL

85 timeless designs from the Design Traditions Library. 160 pgs $17.95 TRA

COTTAGES

25 fresh new designs that are as warm as a tropical breeze. A blend of the best aspects of many coastal styles. 64 pgs. $19.95 CTG

CLASSIC

Timeless, elegant designs that always feel like home. Gorgeous plans that are as flexible and up-to-date as their occupants. 240 pgs. $9.95 CS

CONTEMPORARY

The most complete and imaginative collection of contemporary designs available anywhere. 240 pgs. $9.95 CM

EASY-LIVING

200 efficient and sophisticated plans that are small in size, but big on livability. 224 pgs $8.95 EL

SOUTHERN

207 homes rich in Southern styling and comfort. 240 pgs $8.95 SH

SOUTHWESTERN

138 designs that capture the spirit of the Southwest. 144 pgs $10.95 SW

WESTERN

215 designs that capture the spirit and diversity of the Western lifestyle. 208 pgs $9.95 WH

NEIGHBORHOOD

170 designs with the feel of main street America. 192 pgs $12.95 TND

CRAFTSMAN

170 Home plans in the Craftsman and Bungalow style. 192 pgs $12.95 CC

COLONIAL HOUSES

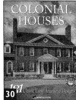

181 Classic early American designs. 208 pgs $9.95 COL

DUPLEX & TOWNHOMES

Over 50 designs for multi-family living. 64 pgs $9.95 DTP

WATERFRONT

200 designs perfect for your waterside wonderland. 208 pgs $10.95 WF

191

ABOUT THE DESIGNERS

Alan Mascord Design Associates, Inc.
Founded in 1983 as a local supplier to the building community, Mascord Design Associates of Portland, Oregon began to successfully publish plans nationally in 1985. The company's trademark is creating floor plans that work well and exhibit excellent traffic patterns.

Design Basics, Inc.
For nearly a decade, Design Basics, a nationally recognized home design service located in Omaha, has been developing plans for custom home builders. Since 1987, the firm has consistently appeared in *Builder* magazine, the official magazine of the National Association of Home Builders, as one of the top-selling designers.

Donald A. Gardner Architects
The South Carolina firm of Donald A. Gardner was established in response to a growing demand for residential designs that reflect constantly changing lifestyles. The company's specialty is providing homes with refined, custom-style details and unique features such as passive-solar designs and open floor plans.

Fillmore Design Group
Fillmore Design Group was formed in 1960 in Oklahoma City by Robert L. Fillmore, president and founder. "Our designs are often characterized by their European influence, by massive brick gables and by high-flowing, graceful rooflines," comments Fillmore.

Home Design Services
Home Design Services is a full-service design firm that has specialized in residential and multi-family design for thirty years. The firm offers a full complement of services, taking a project from concept through completed construction documents. The company's vast experience provides a considerable knowledge of current design trends.

Home Planners
Headquartered in Tucson, Arizona, with additional offices in Detroit, Home Planners is one of the longest-running and most successful home design firms in the United States. With over 2,500 designs in its portfolio, the company provides a wide range of styles, sizes and types of homes for the residential builder.

Larry E. Belk Designs
Through the years, Larry E. Belk has worked with individuals and builders alike to provide a quality product. Flowing, open spaces and interesting angles define his interiors. Great emphasis is placed on providing views that showcase the natural environment.

Living Concepts Home Planning
With more than twenty years of design experience, Living Concepts Home Planning has built an outstanding reputation for its many awardwinning residential designs. Based in Charlotte, North Carolina, the company was founded by partners Frank Snodgrass, Chris Boush, Kim Bunting and Derik Boush. Because of its affinity for glass and design that take full advantage of outside views, Living Concepts specializes in homes for golf and lakefront communities.

Select Home Designs
Select Home Designs has 50 years of experience delivering top-quality and affordable residential designs to the North American housing market. Since the company's inception in 1948, more than 350,000 new homes throughout North America and overseas have been built from Select's plans. Select's design team is constantly striving to develop the best new plans for today's lifestyles.

The Sater Design Collection Inc.
The Sater Design Collection has a long established tradition of providing South Florida's most diverse and extraordinary custom designed homes. This is exemplified by over 50 national design awards, numerous magazine features and, most important, satisfied clients.

Stephen Fuller, Inc.
Stephen S. Fuller established his design group with the tenets of innovation, quality, originality and uncompromising architectural techniques in traditional and European homes. Especially popular throughout the Southeast, Stephen Fuller's plans are known for their extensive detail and thoughtful design.

United Designers & Architects
United Design offers award-winning Ideal Home Plans to builders and consumers worldwide. "At United Design, we know you've got a lot more to think about than plans, so we make it simple. First and foremost, we design beautiful, intelligent homes that appeal to clients of all interests."

Vaughn Lauban
Vaughn Lauban established his design firm in 1976 after working for an architectural firm for twelve years. He wanted a chance to express his own design concepts. Lauban remains diversified in all architectural styles, but he prefers country farmhouses. "I like the simplicity and warmth of these homes, the open floor plans, front porches and softness that says "Welcome to my home." Lauban's philosophy has earned him several awards for some of the top-selling plans in the nation.

Studer Residential Designs, Inc.
Studer Residential Designs was founded in 1971 and specializes in the design of single-family, custom-built homes. The firm enjoys a strong presence in the Greater Cincinnati and Northern Kentucky housing market. In 1992 the decision was made to expand Studer Designs into the national market. Builders enjoy working with a Studer Design because the blueprints are well thought out and easy to read, and simplify the building process.

Northwest Home Designing, Inc.
Northwest Home Designing is a family-owned and operated firm that was founded on a simple principle: create custom home designs that are unique to the needs and desires of its customers. The firm's detailed approach has earned them numerous awards for innovation in design.

Ahmann Design, Inc.
Ahmann Design is a residential design firm specializing in custom residential, stock plan sales, and color rendering. Recognized several times as a finalist in *Professional Builder* Magazine's "Best of American Living" contest, Ahmann Design, Inc. continues to grow as a leader in the residential design market.

Garden Houses of the 1920s
Garden Houses of the 1920s is a collection of classic house plans created and designed by Lew Oliver and Jack Richards, with interiors by Elizabeth Diehl. Seeking to resurrect the ideals of the Arts and Crafts movement, Oliver and Richards create homes with the elegant proportions, sophisticated detail and natural materials of the past while looking to the present and future for inspiration. Design styles include Colonial Revival, Craftsman, Villa Style, and American Vernacular.

Jannis Vann & Associates
Jannis Vann is President and principal designer of Jannis Vann & Associates, Inc. in Woodstock, Georgia. She has been in business since 1982 and has been publishing since 1987. Her collection showcases traditional, country and European exteriors with contemporary, open, flowing interiors.

Greg Marquis and Associates
Incorporating the various features of Southern architecture, the designs of Greg Marquis include emphsis on accurate, detailed drawings and functional floor plans. Greg's designs focus on utilizing space without sacrificing the unique and appealing floor plans which have made his designs so popular.